# The COMPLETE IDIOT'S Guide to

# Buying and Selling
# a Home
## in Canada

- ♦ How to find your dream home
- ♦ Buying and selling - with or without an agent
- ♦ The perfect guide for beginners

**Bruce McDougall &
Shelley O'Hara**

An Alpha Books/Prentice Hall Canada Copublication

Prentice Hall Canada Inc.,
Scarborough, Ontario

**Canadian Cataloguing in Publication Data**

McDougall, Bruce, 1950-
    The complete idiot's guide to buying and selling a home in Canada

Rev. ed.
Previously published under title: The Complete idiot's guide to buying and selling a home for
Canadians / by Shelley O'Hara, Bruce G. A. McDougall, with Maris Bluestein.
ISBN 0-13-897000-9

1. House buying - Canada.  2. House selling - Canada.
I. O'Hara, Shelley. The Complete idiot's guide to buying and selling a home for Canadians.  II. Title.

HD1379.045 1997        643'12        C97-931735-5

© 1997 Prentice-Hall Canada Inc.
Scarborough, Ontario
A Division of Simon & Schuster/A Viacom Company

Prentice-Hall, Inc., Upper Saddle River, New Jersey
Prentice-Hall International (UK) Limited, London
Prentice-Hall of Australia, Pty. Limited, Sydney
Prentice-Hall Hispanoamericana, S.A., Mexico City
Prentice-Hall of India Private Limited, New Delhi
Prentice-Hall of Japan, Inc., Tokyo
Simon & Schuster Southeast Asia Private Limited, Singapore
Editora Prentice-Hall do Brasil, Ltda., Rio de Janeiro

ISBN 0-13-897000-9

Managing Editor: Robert Harris
Acquisitions Editor: Jill Lambert
Copy Editor: Heather Lange
Editorial Assistant: Joan Whitman
Production Coordinator: Julie Preston
Art Direction: Mary Opper
Cover Design: Kyle Gell Art and Design
Cover Photograph: First Light
Interior Illustration: Judd Winick
Page Layout: Gail Ferreira Ng-A-Kien

    2 3 4 5    RRD    01 00 99 98

Printed and bound in the United States of America.

Visit the Prentice Hall Canada Web site! Send us your comments, browse our catalogues, and more.
**www.phcanada.com**

# Contents

# Introduction

Idiots and houses seem to go together. If you own one, you feel like an idiot as you dole out your hard-earned money to pay your taxes, mortgage, insurance, water, hydro, gas, repair and maintenance bills while the value of real estate falls through the floor. If you don't own one, you feel like an idiot for making a monthly rental payment on a place you don't really like but that you don't want to improve at any expense because you don't own it and you may move soon anyway, but meanwhile the price of real estate is going up and soon you won't be able to afford a house anyway even if you can scrape together a reasonable down payment.

Don't despair. Just look around you. Most of the people you see own their own home, including that guy whose shirt collar is caught under his tie and that woman who brings sardine sandwiches to the office in a brown paper bag. If they can figure out how to buy a house, so can you.

## So You Want to Buy a House

You may feel as if buying a house is as hard as riding in the hull of a ship, your children crowded around your feet, with little to eat, awaiting the start of a new life in a strange land. Once you start the house-buying process, you may actually imagine that those obstacles would be *easier* to surmount than the ones you face. With this book, though, you'll find your struggle manageable, sometimes even fun.

*The Complete Idiot's Guide to Buying and Selling a Home* strives to make the home-buying process easier. The book is divided into four parts, each part focusing on a particular step in the process:

**Part I**, "Find Your Dream Home," covers getting ready to buy a house. You have to prepare mentally and financially, and this part tells you what to expect. Part I also covers finding a house—knowing what you want and finding it.

**Part II**, "Make an Offer," covers the offer process. Once you find the house you want, you have to convince the sellers to sell it to you at the price you want to pay. This part covers how to make an offer, review a counteroffer, and get an offer accepted. It also explains the ins and outs of getting financing to pay for the house.

**Part III**, "Close on the House," brings you to the final step: closing on the house. Before you can move in, you have to have a few things done, such as having the house inspected and getting insurance. Then you have the final showdown when you sign a hundred documents, turn over your money, and finally get the keys to your new house.

**Part IV**, "Sell Your House," covers selling your home—making the decision to sell, getting the house ready, deciding whether to use an agent or go it alone, pricing and marketing the house, negotiating offers, and closing on the house.

If you are buying your first home, Parts I-III will lead you through the intricacies of the home-buying market, teaching essential strategies for dealing with real estate agents, lenders, inspectors, building contractors, and other scary people. If you have already bought a house and are now buying a new one, this book can help you, too. During the first purchase, you may have felt like a horse being led around by its nose. "Sign here. You need this. Pay for this." And so on. This book can help you to understand what you are signing, what you need, and what you pay.

## So You Want to Sell Your House

You can use this book to help you through the sometimes difficult process of preparing your home, having it appraised, deciding on an asking price, signing with an agent or deciding to go it alone, and finally, closing on the deal.

If you get through that, you can go back to square one and bone up on the buying process, because in most cases you will turn around and buy another house after you sell yours.

## Extras

In addition to clear explanations and advice, this book offers vital information that can help you accomplish a difficult task more easily or caution you about a common pitfall. These tips are splashed generously throughout the book and are easily recognizable with the following icons:

 Tips mention a better way to accomplish a task, a way to save money, a way to get a better deal, or some shortcut. Read these to get short bits of advice on buying and selling a home.

To avoid common mistakes, look for this pitiful house. Here you'll find warnings and cautions against potential problems and misunderstandings.

### A Bit of Background

These handy sidebars contain useful background information. They also introduce you to the mysterious lingo used in real estate. After reading these, you can throw around terms such as *LTV* and *settlement sheet* like the pros.

# Part I
# Find Your Dream Home

*Owning a home can provide you with many benefits. Once you figure out what they are — or read the rest of this book — you'll likely decide to go ahead and buy one. But first, you need to prepare yourself financially to take the plunge. You have to determine how much you can afford to spend, how big a down payment you can make, and how much you can spend each month.*

*Once you define a price range, you can start looking at homes until you find one that you like. You may fall in love with the first one; or you may look at home after home after home. Somewhere out there, though, you'll find the one for you.*

REAL ESTATE, THE EARLY DAYS

# Chapter 1

# The Dream of Owning a Home

## In this chapter

➤ Understanding the advantages and disadvantages of owning a home

➤ When you shouldn't buy a home

➤ Some home-buying information you may not know

Owning a home is still as enticing as it ever was, but is owning a home right for everyone? Is it right for you? If so, when's the best time to buy a home? When is the worst time? This chapter explores these questions and more.

## This Is a Dream?

When the roof is leaking, your mortgage payment is late, your tax bill arrives in the mail, and your new neighbors move next door in with a 90-pound German shepherd that likes to howl at the moon every night, you may seriously wonder whether buying a home has any advantages. Of course, it does. Here are a few of the important ones:

Home ownership brings with it the advantage of **enforced savings**. Unlike a rent payment, which disappears once you pay it, some of the money you pay on your home goes toward building up your equity. You can take out a loan against your equity, and you usually get back the equity when you sell your home.

If you rent an apartment or house, you don't have too much control over the rent. Your landlord can raise the rent – sometimes as much as he wants. As a home owner, on the other hand, you have the advantage of **fixed housing costs.** If you pay $800 in the first month of a 5-year mortgage, you'll pay $800 the last month, for principal and interest.

Most homes **appreciate**, or increase in value, over time. Yours will likely be worth more when you sell it than when you purchased it. You can use the money you make on the sale of your home to finance a bigger and better home or to finance your retirement. (Keep in mind, however, that not all homes appreciate in value.)

Making timely mortgage payments builds a great **credit history**. If you want to purchase a car or get a credit card, most lenders look favorably on home owners. (So do employers, by the way, who associate home ownership with stable and dependable characters.)

The financial and rational advantages are great. But the biggest advantages of owning a home are emotional: the control and autonomy that ownership affords you, and the sense of pride you take in that ownership. You can paint all the rooms chartreuse and knock out all the walls to remodel if you want. You can add an enclosed porch, install

## How Much Is Your Bucket Worth?

The percentage of the home that you own outright represents your **equity**. When you first purchase a home, the bank owns most of it, so your down payment represents your entire equity. When you start making payments, most of the payment goes toward paying the interest on the loan, but a drop or two goes into the equity bucket. As you pay off more of the loan, more drops go into the equity bucket. When you sell your home, that bucket is yours. To figure out how much equity you have, take the selling price of the home and subtract the amount you still owe on the mortgage. For example, if you sold your house for $100,000 and owed $80,000, you'd have $20,000 in equity.

solar panels or fill the basement with plastic Madonnas with eyes that glow in the dark. It's your house, and you can do what you want.

# Welcome to My Nightmare

Moving to the flip side of the coin, the **disadvantages of buying a home** are mostly financial. You must make the monthly mortgage payments; if you don't, the lender can foreclose on the property and take it away from you. In addition to mortgage payments, you have to pay property taxes and home owner's insurance. Other expenses that you probably don't have as a renter are: all the utility bills (landlords usually cover some, if not most, utilities for apartment dwellers and incorporate the expense into your monthly rent) and maintenance and upkeep on the home and property, such as fixing the leaking roof, mowing the grass, painting the garage, and flushing the squirrels out of the attic. If you live in a condominium, you'll have to cover these expenses in your monthly maintenance payments.

Finally, you can't pull up stakes and leave with a moment's notice if you own a home. If you're a renter, you can give your notice and take off. You don't have any financial responsibilities to the landlord. When you own a home, you have to sell the place before you move on, or make other arrangements to protect your investment.

# Not Now, I Have a Headache

In some cases, buying a home isn't a good idea. When are you better off not buying? Consider these examples:

➤ If you're buying a home solely as an investment, you should be aware that though most homes do appreciate in value appreciation is not guaranteed. Nor can you determine when prices will rise or fall. Many things that you can't control affect the value of your home — the local economy, the national economy, provincial politics, abandoned buildings, new businesses in the neighborhood, a landfill, tacky neighbors who paint their houses chartreuse. Real estate investments can pay off, but so can other investments.

➤ If you know you're going to keep the home for only a short time, because you may be transferred to a new job, for instance, or get married and move, you may want to consider renting rather than buying. When you haven't owned a home for very long, it's difficult to break even, let alone make a profit, when you sell it. You don't have much equity built up, plus you have to pay all the costs of buying and selling the home.

➤ If you don't think you'll like the area where you're considering a purchase, do your homework. Don't just jump in and buy a home because it's, say, close to where you work. Try visiting a block club meeting. Try grocery shopping in the local supermarket, taking your kids to the neighborhood park — anything that will allow you to get to know some of the neighbors and get a feel for the area.

➤ If you can't count on a steady income to make your payments, a lender may not approve you for a mortgage. Even if you get a mortgage, you'll have to make the payments, in full and on time. If you don't, the lender may foreclose. You'll lose all the money you've invested, you'll lose your home, and your credit rating will be ruined, you deadbeat.

### There Is No Perfect Time to Buy

Some buyers get caught in the "I'll wait until I can afford my dream home" trap. These buyers wait and wait until they think the market will be perfect or until they find the house they've always wanted or until they can afford the home they've always wanted. Unless you have a compelling reason to wait, you shouldn't. The perfect market, perfect house, perfect price may not come along. Buy what you can afford, then trade up.

# The Least You Need to Know

Getting ready to buy a home is a big decision. This chapter gave you a basis for making that decision by teaching you that:

➤ There are many advantages to buying a home, including appreciation in the value of your home, enforced savings, and having a place to call your own.

➤ You should carefully consider the wisdom of purchasing a home if you don't plan to live in the area for long, if you're buying the home strictly for an investment, or if you don't have a steady income.

# Chapter 2

# The Up-Front Costs of Buying a Home

> ## In this chapter
> ➤ How much down payment you need
> ➤ What closing costs you have to pay

To acquire almost anything but a headache, you need money. That's what this chapter is all about: money, not headaches. When you buy a home, you should expect to pay out two big amounts — one for the down payment and one for the closing costs. How much you pay for each depends on your particular situation.

This chapter gives you an overview of what you can expect. For more details on financing and closing costs, see Part III.

## Downers: Everything You Need to Know About Down Payments

You'll almost always have to put some money down to purchase a home, even if it's only 5% of the total price. If a purchaser doesn't invest any money of her own in a property, few lenders will give her a mortgage. A purchaser is more likely to walk away from a property in which she has no equity. If she does, the lender has to sell the property to recover the mortgage loan. If property values fall, the lender loses. Even if property values don't fall, the lender has to go to the trouble and expense of listing and selling the property.

Lenders don't like to make risky loans. The more money you put down, the happier (and more lenient) the lender will be.

## How Much Do You Need for a Down Payment?

The size of your down payment depends on many things: the type of financing you want, the amount you can afford to pay per month, and the purchase price of the home.

The down payment is usually calculated as a percentage of the purchase price. The percentage you pay depends on the type of financing you want. (Financing is covered in more detail in Chapter 12 of this book.) A **conventional mortgage** usually covers 75% of the price of a home; the purchaser has to pay the other 25%. If you wanted to buy a home for $100,000, you'd have to pay $25,000 as a down payment.

An **insured mortgage** covers up to 95% of the purchase price. That means the purchaser needs a down payment of only 5%. On a home selling for $100,000, you'd have to put $5,000 of your own money down. You'd also have to pay a premium for the insured mortgage, which is added to your monthly mortgage payment.

## Where to Get the Down Payment

If you already own a home and are moving to a new home, you can probably use the equity from the sale of your first home as the down payment on your second home. If you're a first-time buyer, you may use your savings for the down payment. If you have stocks, bonds, or others assets, you may want to sell these to raise the money for the down payment.

You may have assets that you aren't even aware of. For instance, perhaps you have a stamp collection that you can sell. Or perhaps you have a life insurance policy with some cash value. Consider all sources of income.

The money doesn't have to come from your own savings. It can come from your parents, your high-school physics teacher, or your rich aunt in Nanaimo. The lender doesn't care where you get it, as long as it doesn't affect your ability to repay the lender. Lenders are like that. What can you do? However, if you borrow the money from an institutional lender, using a short-term loan or a second mortgage, it will affect your ability to get the mortgage you want.

## Should I Sell My RRSPs?

If you've scrimped and saved to accumulate money in an RRSP, you may feel tempted to collapse your retirement plan and put the money toward your house. Wise men with beards and degrees will tell you to think twice before you take such a foolish step. But wise men with beards don't have much fun. After you've scratched your head a few times, go ahead and do it.

You'll forfeit the accumulated tax-free earnings of your RRSP-protected savings; you'll have to pay a shockingly high income tax on the money you withdraw; and you'll have to start all over again to save money for your retirement. But you'll also have more money to put down on a house. With a 25-year mortgage, the larger your initial down payment, the more you save in mortgage interest payments.

Presumably your house will also increase in value over the years, or at least maintain its value relative to the rest of the economy. And when you retire, you can sell your house without paying tax on the capital gain, if there is one. Meanwhile, the wise men with beards will still be licking their pencils and scribbling furiously, trying to figure out if you've done the right thing.

## What if You Don't Have Money for the Down Payment?

If you don't have the money for the down payment, you can try one of the following strategies for getting it:

**Start a savings program** and wait until you save 5% or more of the purchase price. If you don't have any savings, you probably aren't ready to buy a home. What have you been spending all your money on anyway? You should have at least a few dollars saved for the down payment. Also, you should be sure that you can afford the monthly payments. So open a savings account now and start saving.

**Consider asking your parents or relatives for a gift for the down payment.** According to a study conducted a few years ago, 31% of all first-time buyers were assisted financially by their parents. If your parents are in a position to help, they can be a valuable resource when you're just starting out.

If you're purchasing a new home, **look for a builder who will consider sweat equity**. In exchange for doing some of the work on the house — painting the interior, for example — the builder may reduce or waive the down payment. Sometimes the builder will issue credits for appliances, carpet, and so on, if you can get a better price from another source.

**Consider using a different type of financing** — for instance, a vendor take-back mortgage (discussed in more detail in Chapter 12).

Consider asking someone to **cosign your mortgage**. This reassures the lender that if you can't repay the mortgage your cosigner can.

All of these strategies are covered in Chapter 12.

Remember, the larger the down payment, the smaller the mortgage on your home. The smaller the mortgage, the less you owe the bank and the more you can keep for yourself to buy that leatherette fold-out couch for the TV room.

## When Do You Fork Over the Down Payment?

When you make an offer on a home, you have to show the seller that you're sincere. An earnest smile and firm handshake won't do it. The seller wants a deposit. The amount required for the deposit varies depending on local practices, the offer you make on the home, and the market (whether it's a buyer's or a seller's market). But it can amount to 5% or more of the purchase price. (The nuances of making an offer are covered in Chapter 8.)

The deposit is held in trust by the realty company and goes toward your down payment. The rest of the down payment is payable at closing. (See Chapter 15 for closing strategies.)

## Closing Time

In addition to the down payment, you'll have to pay some fees and charges when you close on the purchase of the home. Your lawyer will give you an estimate of the closing costs, and you'll probably feel like crying when you see the total. Closing costs depend on local customs and your loan arrangement.

The following chapters will give you an idea of some of the closing costs involved: Chapter 8 considers closing costs as part of negotiating a sale; Chapter 12 shows how to use them for comparing lenders and how to get an estimate of closing costs; and Chapter 15 walks you through actually paying the fees.

# Lender Fees

A lot of money you pay in purchasing a home goes into your lenders' pocket, including:

**Loan application fee** Usually around $200 to $300, this fee is payable when you apply for the loan. However, many financial institutions will waive this fee to win your business. It pays to shop around and to negotiate with your lender.

**Appraisal fee** Before a lender will approve a loan, the home will need to be appraised to see if its value accords with the size of the mortgage you want. In a competitive market, some lenders will waive this fee. The lender usually arranges the appraisal, but you have to pay the

## Paying in Arrears

Mortgage payments differ from rental payments in the way they're applied, which often comes as a surprise to first-time buyers. When you rent an apartment, you pay in advance. On August 1, you pay the rent for the month of August.

When you purchase a house, you pay in arrears. Your payment for August 1 covers the month of July.

When you close on a home, you need to pay for the part of the month that you'll be living in the place. If you close on July 29th, you have to pay for July 29th, 30th, and 31st. You're then paid up for that month. But you don't have to make your next payment until September 1st. It will cover the month of August.

fee, possibly using part of the mortgage loan itself. Expect to pay $150 to $300. See Chapter 12 to learn more about appraisals.

**Survey fee** Lenders want to make sure the property you use as security for your mortgage is all yours to buy. They want to know, for example, that your property doesn't extend into your neighbor's begonia garden or that your driveway hasn't been extended into the public park next door. To reassure themselves, they'll ask for an up-to-date survey. You can sometimes get one from the seller of the property. Otherwise you'll have to hire a surveyor, for a fee of $400 or more.

## Advance and Reserve Payments

All lenders require insurance on the home you purchase. If your spouse sneaks a cigarette in the garage and burns the house down, the lender wants to be sure the damage is covered (more on insurance in Chapter 13). You usually have to pay up front for the insurance and show a receipt and a one-year policy. If you don't, the lender may arrange insurance for you.

Taxes are often included as part of your monthly mortgage payment, as well, especially if you've arranged an insured mortgage. Your real estate agent can give you an estimate of taxes in the area where you're looking for a home. When you're considering a particular house, the listing should indicate the exact amount for current taxes. The listing for a new home, however, will provide only an estimate. If you have any questions, you should check with the local tax office.

If you put down less than 25% for a down payment, you'll have to pay for insurance on the mortgage. It will amount to 0.5% to 3% of the value of the mortgage, depending on the total amount, and is often included in the total mortgage loan.

## Other Fees

You may have to pay other miscellaneous fees. Your lawyer will charge you for the time required to conduct the transaction, prepare the papers, search the title, and perform the other functions required. Usually, lawyers deduct their fees in advance from the mortgage money.

The lawyer's fee includes the **title search**, which ascertains that there are no outstanding liens, unpaid loans, or other claims against the property.

You may also have to pay fees for an **inspection**. The inspector will check for pests, roof damage, problems with the plumbing, wiring, heating, water, structure, and more. Inspections are covered in Chapter 14.

# The Least You Need to Know

Once you've decided to purchase a home, you have to prepare financially. You need to round up some money for the down payment and the closing costs.

➤ You'll have to make a down payment of 25% for a conventional mortgage.

➤ You'll also have to pay closing costs.

# No man acquires property without acquiring with it a little arithmetic also.

## —Ralph Waldo Emerson

# Chapter 3

# Figuring Out How Much You Can Borrow

> ### In this chapter
> ➤ Calculating your total income and monthly expenses
> ➤ Figuring out how much you can borrow
> ➤ Prequalifying for a loan
> ➤ Checking your credit history

If you had enough money to pay in cash, buying a home would be fairly simple: find the house and write the check. Unfortunately, there are very few people who can pay cash for a home. Around 99% of home buyers borrow money to buy their home.

How much you can borrow is the critical question. All lenders will take a close look at your financial situation. This chapter covers the upfront costs of buying a home and then helps you take a close, perhaps painful, look at your financial situation.

## How Much Are You Worth?

Before a lender will give you a mortgage, he'll take a close look at the money you make and the money you spend. So that you're prepared, you should scrutinize your own income and debts.

## Your Income

The first thing you should do in figuring out how much money you can spend on a house is to take a good look at your income. You need to total your annual and monthly gross income (before taxes). To do this, gather all your savings account information and check stubs from the shoe box where you keep them under the empty computer carton in the closet. If you have other income, gather that information also. If you'll be buying the home with a partner — for example, your spouse — gather income information for this person as well.

Keep in mind that lenders will look for an average income. They'll evaluate your income for the past two or three years to make sure that it has been steady and to take into consideration any seasonal jumps. Usually two years' continuous employment will satisfy the lender that you have a steady income. If you've recently graduated from university or college, lenders may take into consideration your future earning power, although they may require a guarantor such as a parent to apply for the mortgage with you.

You'll need a letter of confirmation of employment from your employer if you have a job. If you're self-employed, the lender will usually consider as gross income the amount of money on which you paid taxes, and you'll need your tax returns to prove it. For instance, if your business grossed $100,000, but you paid taxes on only $35,000, the lender will consider $35,000 as your gross annual income. You'll have to show the lender your tax returns for the last three years.

Bonuses don't always count, because this money isn't guaranteed. If you want to have your bonus money considered as part of your gross salary, you need to prove that bonuses are a regular part of your pay. Your employer may write a letter saying that the bonus is predictable.

If you receive alimony or child support, you can include this money in your total, if you want. You must show that this is a reliable source of income. You may need a settlement statement from your divorce that states the amount. Most lenders will consider only income that can be verified — from your employer or from past tax returns.

## Your Monthly Expenses

You know the money that you have coming in. Now you need to figure out how much money is going out. Lenders will also want to know what monthly expenses you have. For conventional loans, lenders don't care that you spend $5 every day to eat at Pizza Hut; they're concerned with long-term debt, which will take you more than ten months to pay off.

You'll need to determine all your required monthly payments — on student loans, for example, or car loans — and total them. This includes payments you have to make on all your credit cards.

# How Much Can You Borrow?

You can use a ballpark method to figure out how much you can borrow. Roughly, you can borrow up to 2½ times your annual salary. If you and your partner make $50,000, you can buy a house in the $100,000 to $125,000 price range.

Keep in mind that ballpark figures don't tell the whole story. For one thing, ballpark figures make a lot of assumptions about your situation. To satisfy a lender, you'll have to take the time to work through the lender's ratios, discussed in greater detail in Chapter 12.

## Use Your Computer

WHOA!

If you have a computer and a spreadsheet program, you can build your own worksheets that determine monthly payments and other calculations.

If you really want to explore all the possibilities, you may want to purchase software designed specifically for buying a home.

# Using a Lender's Ballpark Figure

Lenders and agents are a little leery of the ballpark method. For one thing, this method is too easy, and if they allow things to look too easy, you may figure out you don't need them. More importantly, rough estimates don't reflect individual circumstances. For example, if one couple with a $50,000 income has $20,000 in savings and no car payments, they may be able to afford an even more expensive house than a ballpark figure would indicate. If another couple with a $50,000 income has two car payments and maxed-out credit cards, and they intend to get their down payment by winning the lottery, they might not qualify for a home in any price range.

Lenders compare your income and monthly payments to certain qualifying ratios. You'll see these ratios expressed like this: 28/36 (the

### Maybe. Maybe Not

Just because a lender says you can afford house payments of $1,200 doesn't mean you actually can. On top of the principal and interest, you need to add taxes and insurance. Taxes depend on where you live, and insurance depends on the policy you purchase. You can ask your agent to give you estimates of these payments.

### The Guessing Game

How did they come up with these ratios? Lenders don't like guesses, but that's basically what the ratios are. The lenders feel if they follow these guidelines, home owners will be able to pay off the loan.

ratios most often used for conventional loans). The first number, sometimes called the **front** or **housing** or **Gross Debt Service ratio**, is the percentage of your income you can spend on housing. For example, most lenders say your monthly house payment (including loan payment, property taxes, and insurance) shouldn't total more than 32% of your gross monthly income (that is, your gross annual income, divided by 12). The ratio used depends on the amount of money you put down.

The second number, the **back** or **overall debt** or **Total Debt Service ratio**, totals your housing expenses plus your long-term monthly debt, then figures this total as a percentage of your monthly gross income. For example, most lenders say that your housing expenses plus your monthly debt should not be more than 40% of your monthly income.

# Preapproval: "They Like Me!"

Most banks, trust companies, credit unions, insurance companies, and other lenders will confirm in writing the maximum size of mortgage for which you qualify. This confirmation, called a preapproval, usually remains in effect for 60 to 90 days. It enables you to realistically evaluate the market, focusing not only on homes that you like, but also on homes that you can afford. The lender must still approve the property that you choose. In fact, sometimes the lender may decide that you've paid too much for the property and give you a mortgage for a lower amount than you'd expected.

### Keep Your Head

With an experienced lender and agent, you can sometimes do some creative financing to qualify for a loan. They won't recommend anything illegal, but they may make suggestions about how to lower your monthly debts or how to finance your loan. The point is to be careful not to get in over your head.

# Checking Your Credit Record

Before they approve a loan, lenders evaluate an applicant's business and personal credit history through electronic links to one of Canada's two national credit bureaus. All Canadians who have borrowed money have established a credit history that reflects their repayment habits, current address, and employer's name. This information is gathered from public records and lenders such as financial institutions, department stores, and oil companies.

Before you qualify for a loan, the lender will check your credit record to ensure that you don't have any credit problems. If you have had a history of credit problems, you should be prepared to respond to any questions or problems on the report.

If you haven't been late or missed any credit payments, you probably don't have to worry about getting a bad credit report. But mistakes do happen and sometimes your report may include something that's wrong or a problem that has been resolved. Sometimes your record may reflect the credit history of someone else with the same name. Get a copy of your credit report just to double-check.

### Cut the Cards

If you have several credit cards, get rid of most of them before you apply for a loan. Having too many credit cards may be looked on unfavorably by lenders. With easy access to credit, you could get yourself into trouble.

### Check Your Own Credit

You can obtain your own credit history by contacting the companies that compile such documents. Usually you'll need photocopies of two pieces of identification, along with proof of your current address, taken from a utility bill or credit card invoice. Mail this information to: Equifax Canada Inc., Box 190, Jean-Talon Station, Montreal, Quebec H1S 2Z2 or Trans Union Consumer Relations Department, P.O. Box 338-LCD1, Hamilton, Ontario L8L 7W2. They'll mail the appropriate information to you in about two weeks.

## Correcting a Mistake or Responding to Problems

If your credit report doesn't show any problems, you can rest assured that your loan won't be turned down because of your credit report. If your report does include a problem, you should correct it (if it's in error) or resolve it.

If you have an outstanding debt, resolve it by contacting the creditor. Be sure to send a letter to the creditor asking the creditor to notify all the reporting services and yourself that the problem has been fixed. If you can't resolve the problem, the credit agency must include your explanation of the problem in the credit report.

If your report has a mistake, you need to get the reporting agency to correct it. This is harder than actually clearing an outstanding debt! Write a complaint letter; call the local office. If you can't get resolution, call the bureau manager.

Slow pays are almost as bad as no pays. If you pay your bills, but pay them late, you may think that you don't have a bad record. Slow pays (late pays) reflect poorly on your credit record. You should document or explain any late payments, especially any late rent or mortgage payments.

## The Least You Need to Know

Preparing financially to buy a home can be scary. If you don't figure out in advance how much you can afford, you may get your heart set on your dream home, and then not qualify for the loan, or you may get the loan but be unable to make payments. To figure out the maximum price you can afford, keep these things in mind:

➤ Lenders look at two ratios when deciding whether you qualify for a loan. The Gross Debt Ratio requires that your mortgage payment not exceed a certain percentage (usually 32%) of your monthly

### Bad Debt, Bad Dreams

Your credit history includes information on former loans, mortgages and outstanding credit card balances. It indicates the nature of the loan, how quickly you repaid it, whether a lender has ever turned over a loan to a collection agency, and whether you've ever gone bankrupt. Unfavorable information such as a bankruptcy is kept on file for about seven years. Multiple bankruptcies are recorded permanently.

income. The Total Debt Ratio requires that your mortgage payment plus your total debt payments do not exceed a certain percentage (usually 40%) of your monthly income.

➤ Mortgage payments can consist of the principal, interest, taxes, and insurance.

➤ To find out how much you can borrow, you can ask a lender for a preapproved mortgage.

➤ To prequalify yourself, divide your gross annual income by 12 to get your gross monthly income. Your mortgage payments should consume no more than 30% of this amount.

➤ It's a good idea to check your credit record to ensure you don't have any credit problems. If you do, resolve the problem or have your record corrected before you apply for a loan.

**A man travels the world over in search of what he needs, and returns home to find it.**

**—George Moore**

# Chapter 4

# Picking an Agent

## In this chapter
- ➤ Your real estate scorecard — finding out who's who
- ➤ Who pays the agent?
- ➤ Do you need an agent?
- ➤ Working with for-sale-by-owner homes

When you announce your desire to purchase a home, you may be surprised at the number of real estate people who want to represent you. Agents come out of the woodwork, calling you, sending you information, following you around at open houses, knocking on your door. It may seem like every other person you know turns out to be a real estate agent.

Finding an agent is easy; finding a good one is harder.

## Agents

The agent handles the buying and selling of homes and may also be called a sales associate (or Bart or Betty). An agent is always associated with a broker, sometimes as an employee but more often as an independent contractor. In some cases, the agent has a broker's license, too.

The agent who puts the house on the market or lists the house is often called the listing agent. Your agent, the agent who shows the house and handles the buyer, is often called the buyer's agent or a subagent.

**Negotiate**

If you're listing your own home and looking for a new one through the same agent, the sales commission may be negotiable. Ask your agent. Agents may be willing to lower the commission if they both list and sell the house.

# Who's on My Side?

In the past when you bought a home, everyone worked for the seller — the person showing you homes and the people working with you to find a home. All of these people represented the seller and were paid by the seller — even the buyer's agent. This sometimes came as quite a shock to people buying a home.

The trend is changing, though, and now you can select how you're represented — with a subagent, a dual agent, or a buyer's agent.

## Using a Subagent

The agent who represents you, the buyer, is actually paid by the seller. Here's how it works: when a home is put on the market, the seller agrees to pay a percentage of the selling price to the agent(s) involved in selling the home. Six percent is common. So suppose that a house sells for $100,000. The commission on the house would total $6,000. That money is divided into two parts. The agent who listed the house gets part of the money. This agent splits his pot with his principal broker. The agent who introduces the buyer to the house gets the other half and usually splits his commission with his principal broker, as well. If the listing agent both listed and sold the house, the listing agent and his principal broker split the entire commission.

Unless you have a contract to the contrary (some jurisdictions like Ontario require them), the subagent you choose actually represents the seller and must abide by the seller's instruction (unless the instruction is illegal). The agent must work to get the highest selling price (which is also in his own interest, because he gets a bigger commission). He can't disclose to a purchaser any information that might jeopardize the seller's position.

Even as he drives around a neighborhood with you in the passenger seat, the agent must keep confidential all seller information. The agent, for instance, can't tell you that the sellers are desperate and that they're willing to accept a lower bid, unless doing so is in the seller's best interest.

Nor can the agent tell you what to offer for a particular house or point out defects of a house (unless the seller is trying to hide them, in which case it's his duty to disclose them). However, your agent **must** pass along to the seller any information you say that's of interest to the seller. For example, if you say that you're going to offer $90,000 for the house but you're willing to go to $100,000, your agent can pass along this information to the seller's agent.

## Using a Buyer's Agent

A buyer's agent represents you, the buyer. The agent can make recommendations to you on what price and terms to offer. When the buyer's agent negotiates a deal, she negotiates it with only your interests in mind. Anything you tell the agent is confidential; she won't pass the information along to the seller.

How a buyer's agent is paid depends on the agreement you reach with the agent. Most get a flat fee or a commission based on the purchase price. Some require a retainer that may or may not be applied to the total fee. Some require a minimum fee. Sometimes you pay the fee, sometimes the seller pays the fee.

### Keep It to Yourself

If you work with a subagent, you shouldn't tell the agent how much you're willing to pay for a home. Your agent must certainly know the price range you can afford, but don't tell the agent the maximum amount you'll pay for a property. Don't reveal any special terms you'd consider offering the seller. Don't tell your agent anything you wouldn't want the seller to know.

### Only You

In the past, a buyer could work with more than one agent at a time. But if you sign a contract with a buyer's agent, only one can represent you during a specified period.

You need to know exactly what you'll pay and how much. You may also want to have a cap on the total cost. Finally, you should ask about the retainer. Is it required? Will it be applied to the total fee due? Is there a minimum fee?

### Get It In writing

If you and a seller reach a tentative agreement then decide to change your minds, you'll need your agent's approval in writing to kill the deal, if you have a contract with a buyer's agent.

### Check It Out

If you use a buyer's agent from a bro-kerage firm, be sure to ask how **conflicts of interest** are handled. The firm, re-member, has both types of agents. Also, check into the disclosure rules. Will the firm tell you whether it is a **dual agency**, meaning it is representing both parties?

## Duals

If you have a buyer's agent and she shows you a property listed by the same company, you have a dual agency. The buyer's agent should tell you when this occurs.

# Do You Need an Agent?

Do you need an agent? Probably. The next sections explain some of the benefits you can expect to get from using an agent.

## Financial Help

It would be great if, by financial help, I meant the agent was willing to lend or, better yet, give you the money to buy the house. That would make using an agent worthwhile!

Unfortunately, I mean a different kind of financial help. A real estate agent can help you financially in these ways:

**Analyzing your financial situation**. Your agent can help you answer these questions: How much home can you afford? How much down payment can you afford? What can you do to be in a better situation to afford a home?

**Estimating the costs of home ownership**. In addition to analyzing your financial situation, your agent should also be able to prepare you for the costs of owning a home (mortgage, taxes, insurance, and so on). Also, the agent should be able to translate a mortgage amount into monthly payments. For example, if you purchase a

$100,000 home, what (roughly) will your monthly payments be?

**Educating you about the types of financing**. An agent should be knowledgeable not only about real estate but also about financing. She should be able to explain the different types of financing available as well as what might be appropriate for your situation. If she can't answer all your financial questions, she should be able to put you in touch with someone who can.

**Helping you get and work with a lender**. Some agents can recommend a particular lender and tell you what to expect when you apply for a loan. Some agents may even go with you and help you through the loan application process. Some may help you shop for a loan with the best terms.

# Finding the Right House

In addition to financial assistance, the agent's key role is in helping you find a home. Using an agent has several advantages over just looking yourself.

**Exclusive!**

You'll probably be asked to sign an exclusivity agreement, which says you'll work only with that agent for a specified period (usually 60 to 90 days).

**Open and Closed**

If you walk into an open house without an agent and decide you like the place, the agent conducting the open house automatically becomes your representative.

For example, an agent can help you define what type of home you want by asking you a lot of questions: How big a home do you need? Do you plan to resell the home? What's your family and job situation? Do you have children? Plan to have children? Will you be transferred to another job? By being nosy, an agent can help you get a good idea of what you want.

An agent has access to the Multiple Listing System (MLS), which lists detailed information about most homes for sale in your area. The automation of listing systems makes MLS information in major cities more accessible to the general public. (This topic is discussed in Chapter 6.) But an agent can still help with the nuances of a deal.

A good agent, like a good stockbroker, plays the role of matchmaker, listening to what you want and then helping you find the right house. An agent can search for houses within a particular area, within a particular price range, or with certain characteristics. A good agent will keep up-to-date on the current listings and show you new properties as they're listed.

An agent has information about the community or city where you want to live. If you're moving to a new city, an agent will be extremely valuable. The agent can recommend certain areas, give you an estimate of taxes, tell you about the local school system, community services, hospitals, police, crime, nightlife, and so on.

An agent will arrange appointments for you to visit homes and will tour them with you. From the listing, the agent can tell you a lot about the house — age, lot size, square footage of the entire house as well as each room, listing price, and more. The agent also has the experience of looking at many, many homes and can help you evaluate the quality of the home, compared to price.

**Get Respect**

Sellers take buyers represented by agents more seriously. The seller doesn't have to be nervous about wasting his time on a buyer who can't afford the home.

## Negotiating and Closing the Deal

An agent can be especially helpful in making an offer and negotiating the deal. She'll help you prepare the sales agreement that lists the critical terms of the sale — selling price, terms, contingencies, and so on. She'll represent your offer favorably and will help you handle any counteroffers. Chapter 8 covers the details of making an offer.

The agent will be able to evaluate the property and has access to information about other similar properties. For instance, your agent can tell you the selling prices of other houses in the area. You can often use this knowledge as a bargaining tool.

Even after the offer is accepted, the agent will help shepherd you through the rest of the process—getting the loan, having an inspection done, responding to any problems, and handling the closing. If any problems pop up during the process, your agent will help you through them.

# Selecting a Good Agent

As with most sales jobs, the 80/20 rule applies to real estate: 20% of the agents sell 80% of the homes. When you're selecting an agent, you want one of the 20%. You want someone with experience. This section helps you find an agent you can be comfortable with.

# Finding an Agent

If you've ever gone to an open house, you know how quickly you're besieged with offers to help you find your dream home. The open house agent may follow you around the house, trying to become your agent. Sometimes the agent is more interested in soliciting clients than in showing you the house. You may easily find yourself hooked up with an agent when you had no intention whatsoever of getting involved.

It's better to put some thought into selecting an agent. Don't necessarily sign up with the first person who promises you your dream home. Here are some strategies for finding a good agent:

**Ask others for recommendations**. The best sources of recommendations are family, friends, and coworkers who have recently purchased a home. If someone worked with an agent and had a good experience, chances are the agent is pretty good.

**Ask the broker for recommendations**. The broker should be knowledgeable about all his agents. Ask the broker for the agent who has sold the most in the office. Ask the broker to recommend an agent familiar with the area and price range you want.

**Check the agent's background.** What is the reputation of the firm? Has the firm sold a lot of houses? Does the firm have a lot of agents? Is the support staff friendly? Ask for the agent's résumé.

**Check the agent's history.** How long has she been in business? How long has she been working full time selling real estate? (Some agents work only part time.) How many properties has she listed? (The more the better.) How many properties has she sold in the past few months? Be sure that the agent has access to MLS listings.

**Investigate problems.** Ask the local real estate board whether there have been any problems with the agent.

# Putting an Agent to the Test

Once you select an agent, be sure you enjoy working with that person. You're going to find that the more comfortable you are with your agent, the more pleasant the whole home-buying process is. Take this agent comfort test to be sure you're working with an agent you like.

**Yes  No**

❑  ❑  Does your agent return your calls? Is she pleasant and helpful when you call?

❑  ❑  Does the agent have time for you?

❑  ❑  Does your agent explain things so that you can understand? Does he explain different financing options? Implications of contracts? You want an agent who, first, knows the answers and, second, can explain the answers so that you can understand. You don't want an agent who glosses over the answers, explains things so that you end up more confused, or tells you not to worry about the answers, because he'll take care of it.

❑  ❑  Is your agent interested in your needs? Does she listen to you? You want an agent who listens — not one who's just interested in making a sale.

❑  ❑  Does the agent ask you personal questions about your financial situation? You may think the right answer is no, but the better answer is yes. If you find your dream home and can't afford it, what good is it? An agent should, first, help you figure out what you can afford and, second, help you find homes within that range. If an agent doesn't first investigate your financial situation, you may find yourself in over your head.

❑  ❑  When the agent takes you to look at homes, do they seem to match what you're looking for? If you've stressed to the agent you want a one-storey house, but all she shows you are two-storey houses, the agent may not be listening.

❑  ❑  Does the agent know the area well? Some agents are more familiar with a certain area. You want an agent who knows the area — knows what homes have sold for in the area, knows the taxes, community, etc.

   ❑      ❑      Does the agent show only homes listed with his firm? If so, you might inquire whether the agent gets an incentive if he sells a home with his firm. You want an agent who isn't steering you to certain properties for his own benefit.

## Getting Rid of an Agent

Just because you selected one agent doesn't mean you're stuck with that person for the rest of your house-buying life. You might have chosen an agent spontaneously and then realized this person wasn't right for you. Maybe an agent is too busy? Or too pushy?

If you're uncomfortable with an agent, you should say so as soon as possible. If you've signed an exclusive contract with the agent, read the fine print to find out when you can switch to another agent. You may need the agent's consent or to wait for a specified period.

# Working with For-Sale-By-Owner Homes

When you're looking for a house, you may see a lot of "For Sale By Owner" homes, abbreviated FSBO and pronounced, believe it or not, "fizz-bo." In this case, the seller is not using an agent, and has decided to sell the house directly to you. You and the seller, one on one.

Dealing with a FSBO can be tricky. You can decide to deal directly with the seller, or in some cases you can persuade the seller to work with your agent.

If you decide to deal directly, you'll have to handle all the negotiations between you and the seller, and you'll lack the experience of an agent in helping you write a good contract, get financing, negotiate, and close. Be careful. There are lots of i's to dot and t's to cross in the buying and selling of a house. You need to be sure not to forget something critical in the process. And you should always hire a lawyer to look over all the paperwork.

The seller should be prepared to help you with financing and should handle the closing. The seller may also have a sales contract you can use. But can you trust the seller? If he's handily prepared a contract for you, are you sure he's not salivating and stifling a giggle as you sign your first-born child away?

Be sure that you can handle the stress of dealing face to face with the seller. Sometimes you lose your leverage without a go-between. Face-to-face negotiating can be tough.

Finally, you have to know where your leverage is. For example, the seller, if he sells directly to you, is going to save 6% of the sale price. On a $100,000 home, that's $6,000. Who's getting the savings? If the seller wants to pocket the entire savings, what's your benefit? You should be able to negotiate a lower selling price. Or you may want to insist on using your agent and having the seller pay the 3% commission fee. Or you could negotiate to have your agent do all the paperwork for a flat fee.

# The Least You Need to Know

Selecting a good agent is another step along the way to owning a home. When you're selecting and working with an agent, keep these main points in mind:

➤ An agent can help you prepare financially to buy a home, has access to home listings so that she can help you find a match, and can help you negotiate and close the deal.

➤ You want an agent who is active (sells and lists many homes) and knowledgeable. You also want an agent with whom you feel comfortable and who listens to you.

➤ You shouldn't avoid FSBOs, but you should be prepared to handle some of the special situations that arise from them.

# Chapter 5

# Defining Your Dream Home

> **In this chapter**
> ➤ Understanding how your lifestyle affects your home selection
> ➤ Picking a good location
> ➤ Selecting a house style
> ➤ Deciding on a new home, existing home, or condominium
> ➤ Designing your ideal home

When you shop for anything, it's good to have at least a rough idea of what you want to buy. If you went out to buy a car, but had no idea what type of car you wanted, you could spend weeks or even months making a decision. Sports car? Van? Jeep? Luxury car? Station wagon? Truck? Minivan? Cart and horse?

The same goes for buying a home. Before you start shopping, you should think about what you need and what you want in your ideal home.

## A Few Cautions

This chapter will give you an idea of the elements to consider when you're searching for a home. You shouldn't use this chapter to narrow your house-hunting to a specific property — a split-level red brick home with four bedrooms, two baths (one with a hot tub), country kitchen with pot rack and marble fireplace, entertainment room, two-car garage, asphalt driveway, swimming pool, and yard with privacy fence. If you do, you may not find a home in your price range that matches your dream exactly, and you could miss other homes that you may have liked better.

Instead, use this chapter to picture where you'd ideally like to live. Try to keep in mind that you're probably going to have to compromise. What features are essential? What are extras?

When you go out looking at homes (as described in Chapters 6 and 7), do it with an open mind. Consider what you like and don't like about the home and compare how it matches what you absolutely must have in a house.

Also, trust your agent. If you're working with a good agent (one who listens to what you need), she may recommend looking at homes that vary from your specs. But one of them could turn out to be your dream home.

# This Is Your Life

The first aspect you should consider when shopping for a home is your lifestyle. A retired couple shopping for a home and a newlywed couple shopping for a home will have entirely different sets of needs. This section helps you consider how your family and job affect your housing decision.

### Short Stay

Most people stay in a home no more than seven years.

## Home to Stay or Home to Resell?

Ask yourself how long you plan to stay in the home. If you're buying your first home, will you stay in it for just a while and then move on? If you're planning to move, you should consider the resale value of the home.

On the other hand, if you're shopping for a home in which you plan to live for a long, long time, you should be sure that it will accommodate you for that

## A True Story...

An artist in our neighborhood plans on staying in his house (which was his mother's house) forever. You can tell by looking at the house. For example, he has built a stone doorway with a large wooden owl on the top at the front of the walk. The rest of the yard isn't fenced in, so the doorway opens into an unenclosed yard. He has mounted carousel animals (a giraffe and a swan) on the front porch and an 8-foot troll in the yard. If he planned to sell his house, he probably would have avoided such eccentricities. (I suspect his heirs will be cursing him sometime in the far future, though.)

long, long time. And you may not be as concerned about the resale of the property.

## Is This a Family Home?

Another aspect to consider is your family. Do you have children? Do you plan on having children? If so, you should be sure you have a house large enough to accommodate them. Think not only about right now, but about the future, as well. The cute eight-year-old boy is going to be a teenager before you know it. Is the floor plan suitable for a teenage boy? Where will the kids park once they get that coveted/dreaded driver's license?

Also, consider the location and school district you want to live in. Checking out the neighborhood is covered in the next two chapters.

## What Is Your Job Situation?

Take a look at your job situation. If you're planning to stay in the same job at the same location, consider the length of the drive from your new home to work. What's the maximum amount of time you want to commute? Do you have access to public transportation? Can you quickly get to the highway?

If you're not planning to stay at the same job and location, how will purchasing a home affect your job situation? If you may be transferred soon, will you be able to resell the house quickly?

Also consider your income potential. Will your income go up? Down? Stay the same?

# Location, Location, Location

The three most important factors in buying a home are location, location, location. If you've heard that before, it doesn't matter. It's still true.

Suppose that you find a beautiful five-bedroom home with four baths, a three-car garage, a marble fireplace, a huge kitchen — everything you've ever wanted. What is that home worth? Now think about that same home smack dab next to a garbage dump or in the middle of a high-crime area. What's the home worth now?

The next two chapters give you some advice on how to scope out a neighborhood. Just keep in mind that selecting where you live is more important than selecting what type of house you want.

# Style of House

As you drive down your street, you may look at houses and think, "Who'd want to live there?" There's a particular house in our city that's made of yellow grouted ceramic tile. It reminds me of a big bathroom. To top it off, the house has a rock garden decorated with bowling balls. Every time I drive by the place, I wonder who would pick a house like that. My husband, who has spent the entire summer painting our frame house, finds the house appealing because of the low maintenance. To clean it, you could just scrub it down with some Tilex.

As the saying goes, "To each his own." What you like and what your best friend likes probably won't be the same.

## How Many Storeys?

When you look at houses, you'll find many different styles: one-storey, two-storey, three-storey, split-level, ranch, and so on and so on. What you want and like is up to you. For example, if you're a retired person, you may want a one-storey home so that you don't have to worry about going up and down steps. If you have children, you may want a two-storey house so that you can send the kids upstairs and hide out downstairs. Or you may want the children on the same level as you. You'll have to weigh privacy versus safety.

I've been in a townhouse that had four storeys, which was great if you wanted to get your daily exercise going from the laundry room (first floor) to the kitchen (second) to the office area (third) to the bedrooms (fourth). Forget about the Stairmaster!

## To Paint or Not to Paint

What is the home made of? Is it a wood frame house? A combination brick and frame? Aluminum siding? Stucco? Hay? Sticks? Brick?

Again, selecting what you want will depend on what you like and how much maintenance you want to do. Also, consider the cost of maintenance. Frame houses will require painting; brick houses don't, but sometimes need to be repointed (bricks fixed), which can be expensive. Price will also be a factor. For example, a brick home may cost more than a similar frame house.

As long as the home has been well maintained, you shouldn't have too many worries. You should inquire about the maintenance and keep in mind what you will have to do to keep up the exterior.

# Age of the House

When you're shopping for homes, you have to decide whether you want an existing home or a new home. You may also consider purchasing a condominium. Each type of dwelling has its advantages and disadvantages.

# Existing Home

Most home buyers purchase an existing home rather than a new one. There are many good reasons to purchase an existing home:

Most existing homes are in an **established neighborhood**, usually closer to the city. You can expect to find trees and sometimes larger yards.

An older home tends to have more **personality**. In a new subdivision, you may see several different house styles, but the houses may all look alike. (This will vary depending on the subdivision and type of new homes.) In an older neighborhood, the style and size of the houses

### Times They Are a Changin'

A hundred years ago, most people had only a set of work clothes and a set of church clothes, so closets were understandably small. Luckily, they used the space they saved to build more bedrooms. A creative solution to the Tiny Closet Syndrome is to use one or more of the leftover bedrooms as a spacious, walk-in closet.

will vary. You might have a colonial brick house next to a frame Cape Cod next to a ranch. The older home may also have nice amenities such as hardwood floors or built-in cabinets, which, I can assure you, you'll pay dearly for in a new home.

You may get **more space for your money** in an older home. You'll usually find that the ceilings are higher and the rooms are bigger than in a new home. This won't be true in every case.

On the down side to buying an existing home, consider these factors:

Either women back then didn't have as many shoes as they do now or they had no say in the design of the home, because most older homes have **little, tiny closets** that will hold about three pairs of pants, three shirts, one coat, and three pairs of shoes. And that's for both you and your spouse. You may find that the bathrooms are small, too.

As the home gets older, it's going to require more **maintenance**. You may need to paint the house, fix the plumbing, do rewiring, and more.

With a good inspection (covered in Chapter 14), you can be sure you aren't getting a house that will become a money pit. If repair work does need to be done, you will know about it ahead of time if you get an inspection.

## New Home

As your city expands, you will find that new subdivisions will pop up all over town with brand-new homes and big closets. Consider the following benefits of owning a new home:

Because the heating, plumbing, wiring, air-conditioning, and so on are all new, you'll have the advantage of **low maintenance costs**. Also, the home may be more energy efficient, and the builder will most likely offer a warranty for the major components.

Builders must have perked up and listened to what people wanted in a house because most new home designs include **big closets** and lots of

## Is a Fixer-Upper for You?

Should you buy a fixer-upper? You may think that's the ideal situation. You can buy the house cheaply and then make a bundle after you fix it up. Beware!

If you intend to fix up a home, keep in mind that the repairs and renovations will always cost more and take longer than you anticipated. You should be sure that you can live with the mess. Do you want to take a shower in the basement for the next five years while your spouse redoes your master bathroom?

If you're handy, you may plan to do the work yourself. Most buyers do. But usually, they have to hire someone to finish the job. You should be sure you have the expertise and the time to do the repairs. The work is going to take longer than you think anyway and may end up being endless if you don't have the time to devote to it.

cabinet space. New homes also usually include a well-designed floor plan — big kitchen, special amenities such as a master ensuite, and so on.

When you purchase an existing home, you have to either keep the red velvet wallpaper and black shag carpet or pay the price to redo them. With a new house, you have **more choices**. The builder will usually let you pick the color and type of floor coverings and wall coverings.

Many new subdivisions include **extra amenities for the community**, such as a clubhouse, swimming pool, tennis court, and other fun things.

If you're thinking of purchasing a new home, you will also want to consider the disadvantages:

New homes are being built **farther out in the suburbs** than existing neighborhoods. They may also lack decent landscaping — at least until the trees and grass grow in. Most people are put off by this **barren look**.

If you have your home custom-designed and custom-built, you can select any type of home you want. But most new homes are predesigned by the builders. You can select home A, B, or C. There will be several homes in your neighborhood that look exactly like yours — at least

**Save the Trees**

Most builders just clear-cut all trees from the lot before you ever see it. But if there are trees still standing when you pick your lot, you may want to discuss with your contractor the possibility of leaving some of them. You could negotiate to give up something else if you can keep some trees.

from the outside. This **lack of personality** has kept many people in the existing home market.

Land is expensive. Builders want to fit as big a house on as small a lot as possible. If you hate to mow the lawn, you're in luck. If you don't want to sit on your deck and stare directly into your neighbor's kitchen, you may be out of luck. **Small yards** are part of the bargain with a new house. Also, you may have to put some work into actually getting a yard. You may have to reseed and water until a decent lawn grows in.

In some cases, a new home costs more than an equivalent existing home. Also, you may have **less bargaining power** on the price when you buy a new home. The ins and outs of making an offer on a new home are covered in Chapter 10.

## Condominium

Another type of home you may want to consider is a condominium. When you purchase a condominium, you own the actual living unit, which may be similar to an apartment. You also own a percentage of the common area — building and land. Also, you don't have to worry about home maintenance. Usually, you pay a condo fee for the upkeep of the grounds and the building. Some condominiums include extra amenities such as a swimming pool, clubhouse, and so on. Purchasing a condominium is covered in detail in Chapter 11.

## The Home Itself

So far you should have thought about how long you want to live in the home, who's going to live in it with you, where you want to live, and what type of house you want. Finally, it's time to think about the house itself.

## Eating

The most important area of the house is probably the kitchen. Everybody has to eat. If you like to cook or entertain, you may want to put a big kitchen on the top of your must-have list.

If you have children, you may also want to have an eat-in kitchen — where Junior can throw his Spaghettios as far and as often as he wants without ruining the dining room carpet and table.

In addition to a kitchen, you may want a dining room. (Sometimes the kitchen is both.) The size and style of the dining room will depend on what you like.

**Bedroom Plus**

Bedrooms are for more than just sleeping. They can provide office space, storage space, hobby rooms, whatever.

## Sleeping

What's the first thing you want to do after eating a big meal? Take a nap. The number and size of bedrooms is next on the list of things to consider in a home.

How many bedrooms do you want? How big do you want them?

I've been in a four-bedroom house where the fourth bedroom was so small you'd have to sleep standing up. When you consider the number of bedrooms, remember your family situation. Do you have children? Will you have children? Will you have more children? Will you need to take in an aging parent sometime down the road? Do you have guests frequently?

## Getting Clean

The big three for home selection are kitchen, bedrooms, and bathrooms. The more bathrooms the better. You should decide on the minimum number of bathrooms you need. One? (Good luck!) One and a half? (Be sure the half is big enough for a person. Sometimes people convert a closet into a bathroom. If you can barely fit four outfits in the closet, how do you expect to fit a 5-foot 11-inch person?) Two? (Two is the recommended minimum.) Three or more? (You're living like a king.)

## Relaxing

Okay. You eat, you sleep, and you go to the bathroom. What else do you do in your home? You will want to be sure you have an area to relax, entertain, work, work out, and so on.

Most homes have a living room. Sometimes this is a formal room where no one actually does any living and the furniture is covered with plastic. It looks good, but no one is allowed in. Sometimes the living room is a living/family room where you watch TV, entertain, and lie on the couch.

Some homes have both a living room and a family room or a combination living/family or living/dining room. The family room may be called different names — great room, rec room, den, pig room (that's what my aunt calls it — she has two teenagers). The family room may be used for watching TV, or it may be used as an office. (Sometimes a spare bedroom is converted into an office.) You will want to consider the number and size of the living rooms you need.

## Storing Stuff

I often wonder, if I didn't have a basement or an attic, would I keep so much stuff? In my parents' basement, for instance, you'll find cabinets of dusty toys and games including a broken EZ-Bake Oven, a toy chest full of mildewy old dolls, all my old term papers, trunks of clothes including my Catholic high-school uniform, and much, much more. Do we need any of this stuff? No. But every time my dad threatens to throw it out, my mom and I have a fit. (Plus, we threaten to get rid of his train set, which is also down in the basement.)

When you're thinking about your dream house, think about where you're going to put all your stuff. Do you need a basement? Basements add up to 50% more room to a two-storey and 100% more room to a ranch home. The basement can serve as a storage area, a place to put your washer and dryer, or a place to stick your teenager until he outgrows puberty. And a basement can add to the resale value of the house. Many people move only because they lack a basement.

Your house may also include extra storage space in an attic or storage shed. (Garages are covered in the next section.) Of course, don't forget closets.

## Outside the House

By now, you should have a good idea of what the inside of the house should look like. Now let's take a walk around the outside of the house. What's important to you here? Consider these questions:

**Do you want a little yard, big yard, no yard?** I've been in houses with no backyards, with the backyard at the side of the house (it was very hard to get your bearings in this house), and with a backyard as big as a football field. My husband liked the football-field-sized yard until he thought about mowing it.

**Does the house have a nice view?** A good view can provide you and your family with many years of pleasure, as well as increase the value of the home.

**Is the yard fenced in?** Do you need a fence to keep Falstaff, your bulldog, in the yard? Your kids in the yard? Do you want a fence just for decoration, such as a split-rail fence, or for privacy, such as a ten-foot fence around your swimming pool? Can you add a fence? Is it against local zoning laws? Neighborhood covenants or ordinances?

**Is there room for the kids to play?** Will there be room for their swing set, tree house, and umpteen bicycles and scooters?

**Do you like to garden?** If so, is there room for one? Is the terrain right for a garden? Is it too rocky? Too sloped?

**Where will you park?** On the street? In a driveway? In a garage? How big is the garage? Can you use the garage to store all the stuff that won't fit in your basement: bicycles, sports equipment, yard and gardening tools?

**Does it have a driveway?** Is it gravel? Paved? Does it need to be paved? Is it flat or on an incline? Think about driving down or up the driveway after an ice storm. Can you add a basketball hoop?

## Heating, Cooling, and More

You should think about heating and cooling. Is it important to you whether it has gas heat or electric, radiators or steam? Do you want air-conditioning? How expensive would it be to add central air? Can you rely on window air conditioners? Is the house on city water or well water? Who picks up the trash?

## Amenities

This section covers some of the other "goodies" you may want your house to have. Make a separate list of "must haves," and "would love to haves." Here are some ideas:

➤ Does it have a deck? Can you build a deck?

➤ How about a hot tub? Swimming pool? Tennis court?

➤ Do you want a fireplace? Hardwood floors? Built-in cabinets?

# Definite No's

In addition to thinking about what you want, also think about what you don't want. For example, I hate a house where a cat has lived because I'm allergic to cats. Even if the carpet is shampooed, I can smell the cat, and I sneeze and sneeze and sneeze.

Also, remember that some of the things you hate can be changed. Just because you hate the living room wallpaper doesn't mean you shouldn't buy a house that you otherwise like. On the other hand, it's usually not wise to buy a three-bedroom house when you need a four-bedroom, thinking it will be easy to "knock this wall out and add another room right here." Be sure to consider the difficulty and expense of the changes you'll want to make.

# The Least You Need to Know

Before you go house hunting, you should have in mind a general idea of the type of house you want. This chapter helped you define your dream home by focusing your attention in these areas:

➤ Think about your lifestyle now and in the future. Factors such as whether you may be transferred to another job or whether you plan to have children will affect your housing decisions.

➤ Buying an existing home usually means a more established neighborhood and unique home design. On the down side, expect to have less closet space and higher maintenance costs.

➤ When you buy a new home, you can expect lower maintenance and a better floor plan. The location and lack of personality and yard are drawbacks.

➤ The three most important rooms to consider are the kitchen, bedrooms, and bathrooms.

# Chapter 6

# Finding Houses on the Market

**In this chapter**

➤ Knowing what to expect when you're looking for a house

➤ Finding a house

➤ Finding a good neighborhood

"For Sale" signs are like wildflowers; they crop up all over the place every spring. You can almost hear them as you drive through the neighborhoods in your city: pop, pop, pop.

Why do a lot of homes go on the market in the spring? Is that the best time to shop? Find out the answers to these questions and more right here.

## What to Expect When Looking for a Home

What should you expect when you begin to look for a home? How long will the process take? When is the best time to shop? This section covers these questions, and more.

## How Long Does It Take?

Finding the right home is a lot like dating. The first one could be your dream house. Or you could have to go through a lot of duds before you find your princely estate. The entire process of looking, making an offer, financing, and moving can take anywhere from a couple of months to over a year.

Here's a rough schedule for home buying:

1. You begin by looking for a home that you like. This process can take a few weeks to several months. A 1991 U.S. survey found that the average buyer spent 16 weeks looking for a home. You should start looking as soon as you think you want to purchase a house. If you have to move because of a job transfer or because you've sold your house, you could be in a weak bargaining position if you need a house right away.

2. After you've found the house, you make an offer. The offer is accepted either right away or after a series of counteroffers. Plan on a couple of days for this process. If the offer isn't accepted, go back to the first step.

3. You secure financing for the house. Your contract will probably stipulate that you must apply for a loan within a couple of days. Then the lender must approve the loan. Better still, get a preapproved mortgage before you start looking for a house.

   During the financing phase, other key steps occur. The house may be inspected and appraised. If the seller agrees to make repairs, these must be made before closing. A title search will be done.

4. Your loan is approved, you close on the house, and finally get the keys. Count on a week for this step.

If you're selling your house, you should probably put it on the market before you start looking for another one. If you find a house you want, the seller might not take you seriously if your house is not already on the market or already sold. It's a balancing act. It's nice to sell your house and buy your new house at the same time so you can move from your old house to your new house. If you find a house before you sell yours, you may lose it to a buyer who can close immediately. On the other hand, if you sell your house before you find a house and the buyers want to move in right away, you'll have to arrange for temporary housing.

# Buyer's Market Versus Seller's Market

Depending on the economy, you may find yourself in a buyer's market in which the buyers get the best deals, or you may find yourself in a seller's market in which the sellers get the upper hand. Sometimes, you'll find yourself somewhere in between.

In a buyer's market, there are a lot of homes available, and they may take a while to sell. To sell a house, the seller needs to list it at a really good price, with additional incentives such as help with financing. If you're buying a home in this type of market, you can take your time looking and can usually strike a pretty good deal.

In a seller's market, houses aren't on the market for long. In fact, they may sell before they're even listed. Because the market is so strong, many owners will decide to sell their homes themselves; you'll see a lot of for-sale-by-owner homes. If you're selling a house in this market, you're lucky. You'll probably get many good offers, and you won't need to offer any additional incentives. If you're buying a house in this market, you may have to work hard to find a house that you like, you can afford and you can offer to buy before it's sold (see "Finding a House," later in this chapter). To get your offer accepted, you should be financially ready (prequalified). Also, don't expect to submit and have accepted a contract with a lot of contingencies.

# Seasonal Sales

If you charted the sales of homes for the months of January to December, you'd probably find that it followed a bell pattern. Sales are slow at the start and end (January and December) of the year and peak in the middle (May and June).

These seasonal peaks make sense. Most people don't want to move during the holidays (November to January), so there may not be a lot of homes on the market during this time. Plus, houses don't look as appealing in the dreary days of winter. The trees are bare and the skies are dark.

But winter is a great time to buy. If you're looking for a bargain, consider shopping during the down time. Many homes on the market in this season have to be sold. Otherwise, the sellers would wait for a better time.

Homes look nice in the spring, and it's easy to work on repairs at this time. So you'll see lots of folks out on ladders and lots of homes for sale from March through April. The peak of home buying occurs somewhere around May and June — that's a good time to move if you have children in school, but also may be the worst time to buy. You have a good selection, but the market moves fast.

Sales tend to drop off at the end of the summer — again, children are heading back to school, and parents may not want to uproot them. You may see more houses on the market in September and October, but once the holidays come up, sales drop.

If you have the luxury of shopping when you want, you can use these sale seasons to your advantage.

# Finding the Right Place

You already know that the most important decision you make about where to live is where to live. This section starts by moving from the bigger area (the community) to the smaller area (the neighborhood). The dictionary defines community as "a social group of any size whose members reside in a specific locality, share government, and have a cultural and historical heritage." The concept of community, then, encompasses the services offered in the area (hospital, fire department, and so on) as well as social aspects (shopping, community entertainment centers, and so on).

A neighborhood is more loosely defined as "a number of persons living near one another or in a particular locality." Often the character of the district defines the area, and neighborhoods tend to retain their basic character over long periods. If you think of your town, you can probably think of several neighborhoods and their associated character. For instance, one neighborhood may call to mind local artists and little boutiques and restaurants. Another may call to mind the theme from *Deliverance*.

**Rely on the Agent**

If you're moving from another town or province, you'll have to rely on your agent to provide you with information about different communities and neighborhoods.

## Finding the Right Community

What's the right community? Depends on who you are and what you want.

If you're most interested in living in today's hot community, look for one that's about to have a growth spurt — where the resale value of the home is likely to go up. You can spot promising growth by looking for the construction of new homes, new roads, new community services, new businesses.

If you're more interested in the social aspects of the community, check out the local shopping malls, libraries, churches, and community centers.

If you have children, consider the school district. (Even if you don't have children, living in a good district can improve the resale value of your house. The school district is one of the most significant factors for evaluating a community.)

No matter what your situation, you should choose a community that has good police and fire departments. You should also consider the commuting distance to work.

If you don't want to finance the new school gymnasium or end up living next to a Taco Bell, you should investigate any plans for improvements. How will they be financed? Are any zoning changes coming up?

To get a feel for a particular community, read the local newspaper. What types of stories are covered? What is the attitude of the paper? What about the Letters to the Editor? What are the views of the community leaders? This information can help you decide whether you'll feel comfortable in a particular community.

Visit the community and stop by local stores, libraries, and community centers. Are the stores prosperous? Inviting? Are the people pleasant?

Talk to local residents. Do they work in the area? Or do they commute to another location? What do they like about the community? What do they dislike? How long have they lived in the area? The community is really a reflection of its residents, so the more you know about them, the better sense you will get of the community.

Your agent should be able to give you information about particular communities — statistics about home sales, crime rate, schools, taxes, and more.

Check with the Chamber of Commerce and other associations for information about population and income trends. For instance, you can check with the Homebuilder's Association to find out which areas of the town have seen the most growth.

## Finding the Right Neighborhood

Within each community, you may find several different neighborhoods. Just as you check out the community, you should check out the neighborhood. Ask yourself the following questions:

*Are there a lot of homes for sale in the neighborhood?* A lot of homes could be a good sign — a hot market. Or it could be a bad sign — people trying to get out.

*Are the homes well kept, well maintained?* Or are the homes in need of repair?

*Is the neighborhood close enough to your relatives?* Or, depending on your family situation, far enough away? Do you have access to public transportation?

*Can you characterize the lifestyle of the neighborhood?* And if so, do you fit in? If you have children, for instance, you may want to select a neighborhood with other young families. Are there a lot of swing sets or bicycles? If you're a swinging single, you may want to find a neighborhood where the singles swing.

*Do you see any problems in the neighborhood?* Check at the local police station for information about the crime rate. Look for any negative aspects of the neighborhood — heavy traffic, graffiti, unkempt houses, pollution.

Ask your estate agent for information about home sales in the neighborhood. How many homes have been sold in the past year? How long did they take to sell? What was the difference between the listing price and the selling price for the homes?

**Gadzooks!**

Be sure to check for toxic waste and radiation. You can have some of these tests done as part of the home inspection.

## Finding a Home

You've narrowed down the community and neighborhood to a few choices. Now you can begin to look for a home in one of those areas. How do you find a home? There are many ways, as described here:

# Drive-Bys

As you take a look at the community and neighborhoods you like, you should keep your eyes open for homes for sale. Most homes on the market display a for-sale sign in the yard. Jot down the address and listing realtor of any homes that catch your eye. Write down the numbers of any for-sale-by-owner properties.

# Local Papers

You can also find homes by reading your local paper. You can read the paper's real estate ads and mark homes that sound interesting. If you're just starting to look, visit a few open houses in the area where you want to live.

If you're searching for a bargain, look for words such as reduced or motivated sellers. These terms may indicate the house has been on the market for a while.

Words and phrases such as fixer-upper, TLC needed, handyman special, or needs updating indicate the home isn't in the best condition. If you don't want to worry about repairs and redecorating, look for houses described as in move-in condition.

# MLS Listings

Ninety-five percent of all homes on the market are listed with an agent. And when a home is listed with an agent, information about the home is entered into a computer system known as the *multiple listing system* or *MLS*.

Basically, the MLS listing includes the following information:

➤ The top section includes the two most important pieces of information — the address and listing price. This section also includes information about the location of the property: town, area, township, lot number, and map coordinates.

➤ The next section includes information about the type and size of the rooms — living room (LR), dining room (DR), kitchen (KT), family room (FR), bedrooms (MB, 2B, 3B, 4B, 5B). This section also includes information about the first mortgage, first mortgage payment, taxes, tax year, assumption information, and school district.

➤ The next section includes directions to the home as well as a short summary of the property.

➤ The next section includes a description of the property — style of house, number of rooms, type of exterior, and so on.

➤ The last area includes information about the listing agent — name, phone number, listing date, expiration date of listing, commission.

**Why's He Selling?**

You can get the best deal when the seller is highly motivated to sell — for instance, in special situations such as transfers, divorce, and so on.

If you're working with an agent, she should be able to provide you with lists of homes in a particular price range and in a particular area. Most likely your agent will pull several listings from the system and take you by the homes. If you're interested in a home, the agent will set up an appointment to tour it.

Most often, the agent will accompany you — even when you're just driving by the houses. Sometimes you can convince the agent to give you the listings so that you can drive by yourself.

## Word of Mouth

In a seller's market, houses may sell even before they're listed in the computer system. In this type of market, you may have to be more aggressive in finding a house. Also, the best time to purchase a home is before it is put on the market — when the seller is thinking about selling. If you can catch the seller at this critical point, you may be able to negotiate a good deal. The seller will avoid the hassle of putting the house on the market, and you'll get a house you want.

To find houses about to be put on the market, tell family, friends, coworkers, and acquaintances that you're looking. Any one of these people may know of a house about to be sold. For instance, your friend Pam might know that your mutual friend Steve is getting a divorce and will be selling his house soon. Your mother might know that Cousin Billy is about to be transferred to Vancouver and will be putting his house on the market.

# Auctions and Foreclosures

If you really want a bargain, you should search for an "as-is" or fore-closed property. Look for advertisements in the paper or call some local lenders and ask whether they handle foreclosed properties; if so, how can you get information about the homes?

If you're thinking about buying this type of property, do a title search. Find out before you close if any back taxes are due or if there are any liens against the property.

Foreclosed properties may not have been well maintained; there-fore, commission a careful, professional inspection so that you know about any problems or costly repairs that are needed.

When you're at an auction, be sure that you understand the rules. You may be required to have a certified cheque ready for the deposit, and you'll most likely need to be prequalified for a loan. Your bidding card may include information about the maximum financing for which you're qualified. Also, be sure you understand when the sale is final. Some auctions take the highest bid — no matter what. Other auctions have a minimum bid. Some auctions require the sale to be confirmed by the seller before it is final.

Be careful not to overbid. Do your homework and decide on the market value for the house as well as how high you'll bid. If you get into a bidding war, stop at your maximum price. Otherwise, you may end up paying far more for the house than you intend.

**Bidder Beware!**

Buying a home from an auction is not for the novice. This process requires great care and caution. You need to be experienced in home-buying — know what to pay for a certain property and how the process works. You could ask your agent to act as a bidder for you in an auction.

# What to Expect in the Near Future

In the past, agents have had a stranglehold on the MLS listings. A person working on his own couldn't get access to the listings without the help of an agent. With computers and the Internet, people can gain access to this information directly.

Some realtors allow house hunters to gain access via modem and computer to their database of homes for sale (the MLS). Some firms provide access to a computer bulletin board of homes for sale.

Some agencies have access to online information about homes. For instance, your agent may be able to show you six to eight different color pictures of the home right on your PC screen. You can view 50 to 100 homes in about an hour and narrow your choices considerably before venturing out. If you don't have access to a computer and a modem, you may be able to use your touch-tone phone to dial in and get information about homes for sale.

In the future, virtual reality systems will enable you to visit a home electronically without actually going there. You could visit the rooms, check the closets, inspect the exterior — without ever leaving the real estate office.

# The Least You Need to Know

House hunting is like searching for a lost treasure. You need to follow maps, decode secret messages, and use your best sense to find the treasure. In your search, keep these things in mind:

➤ To buy a house, you need to go through four steps: find the house, have an offer accepted, finance the purchase, and close. There's no time limit for these steps — it varies wildly.

➤ Check out the community by reading the local paper, visiting community stores, talking with residents, and driving around.

➤ Neighborhoods come with their own unique characteristics. You should choose a neighborhood in which you feel comfortable.

➤ You can find houses on the market through your agent, by reading the local paper, by driving through neighborhoods you like, and by word of mouth.

# Chapter 7

# Looking At a House

> ## In this chapter
> ➤ Touring the house
> ➤ Deciding whether the house fits you
> ➤ Ensuring the house meets your needs
> ➤ Making sure the house is well maintained
> ➤ Checking the neighborhood
> ➤ Keeping notes

A recent survey showed that the typical home buyer looks at 15 to 19 homes before making a decision. When you're looking, how can you keep all the homes straight? What are you looking at in each of these homes? This chapter gives you some strategies for taking a good look at a house, for checking the neighborhood, and for keeping all the houses straight.

## What to Expect

Your agent will do her best to match your needs to houses currently on the market. She may drive you by some homes and then set up appointments for the ones you find appealing. Or she may set up appointments for houses she thinks you will like. You could have several appointments in one evening or day.

When you tour a home, the agent will accompany you, but the home owners may or may not be in the house. Your agent will also most likely give you an information sheet that tells you the age of the house, square footage, size of rooms, property taxes, utility bills, and so on. The information sheet may also include a picture.

As you tour the house, you may want to jot down notes. If you have any questions, ask your agent. If she doesn't know the answer, she can usually find out. For instance, you might ask when the roof was replaced or what type of plumbing is in the house.

If you can easily revisit the house, you may not have to remember exactly how the house looks. If you're moving from another town and can't easily return, take a camera and snap pictures or sketch floor plans.

As you look at more houses, pick one that's the house to beat — the best house you've seen so far. If you compare another house to this one, and it doesn't hold up, forget about it. If you compare a house and it's better, forget about the first one.

After you look at several houses, you may want to return to one. Keep in mind that you shouldn't waste the seller's time.

The rest of this chapter gives you some suggestions on what to look for as you tour.

## Tips on Remembering

*Look at just a few houses at a time.* If you look at ten or more, the homes will quickly become a blur.

*Pick a nickname for the house you want to remember.* Maybe it's the "baby blue," the "cat house," the "new baby home."

*If you have a video camera, take it along and videotape the home.* Be sure to get permission to do so first.

## Do You Like the House?

If everyone had the same tastes, all the homes on your street would look the same. Instead, all homes are different, and each person has different likes and dislikes. The first thing you have to decide about a house is if you like it.

Sometimes you'll have an immediate reaction to a house. It just feels right. "This is my house," you may think. Sometimes you may take a while to warm up to a house. As you go through it, you may hear a little voice saying, "Yeah, yeah." Other times you'll immediately hate a house.

Why the intense emotions? Because your home is a reflection of you. Some homes fit, some don't. There's no way to predict an individual's reaction. You just have to gauge yours.

### More Than One

You may think there's just one home that's perfect for you, but there are probably several. Keep your perspective. If a deal doesn't go through on that perfect home, rest assured that you'll find another one that you'll like just as well.

## Does the House Like You?

After noting the emotional appeal of the home, check out what the house has and what it lacks. Walk through each of the rooms. Keep in mind that you're going to have to be flexible and compromise on some features. Here are some questions to consider:

*Does the house have enough bedrooms to accommodate your family now?* Five years from now? Can you add on?

*Does the house have enough bathrooms?* Are the bathrooms big enough? Can you add a bathroom? If so, what would be the cost?

*Is the kitchen adequate for your needs?* Is there enough counter space? Cupboard space? Are the range and refrigerator included in the sale of the home? If so, are they in good condition? All built-in appliances are usually included; others are negotiable.

*Does the house have enough living space?* Room to work? Watch TV? Relax? Can the living space be adapted to meet your needs in the next five years? For instance, if you're planning on having a child, will there be room for the child to play?

*Does the house have enough storage space?* Check the attic, basement, garage, and closets.

*Are the yard and landscaping acceptable?* Is the lawn overgrown or bare? Will it require work? Do you care how the lawn looks?

*Does the home have the amenities that you want?* Hardwood floors? Built-in cabinets? Fireplace? Deck? Patio?

*What personal property is included with the house?* The washer? Dryer? Dishwasher? If these items are included, are they in good shape? If they aren't included, keep in mind that you may need to purchase the items separately.

## Can You Live in the House?

The best home isn't necessarily the home equipped with everything you want; the best home is the one you like living in. Once you're sure the home has the basic features you need, imagine living in it. For example, you might think a house is okay because it has four bedrooms, and you need four. But how are the four bedrooms situated? Are they next to each other so that you can hear your 14-year-old's headbanger music from your room? Are the bedrooms big enough? Can your eight-year-old fit her entire Barbie collection in her room? As you walk through the house, imagine it's your home. Think about the things you'll do there:

*Imagine your daily routine.* Where will you sleep? Watch TV? Cook? Eat?

*Imagine your entire family in the house.* Where will your children sleep. Are their rooms close enough to yours that they feel safe, but far enough away to have some quiet? Where will your children do their homework? Watch TV? Where will your spouse or you work?

*Walk through the house and check the traffic pattern.* Do you have to walk through five rooms to get to the family room? Are the bathrooms easily accessible for you and guests? Or will your guests have to traipse through your bedroom to get to the bathroom?

*Think about your lifestyle.* Will you have enough privacy? Where will you entertain? If you have guests over, where will they sleep?

*Think about all your possessions.* Where will they fit? Where will you keep your 50-plus pairs of shoes? Your tool collection?

**Try It On for Size**

Taste the water and stand in the shower. These are two things I routinely do when I visit a house. Water tastes different depending on whether it's city water or well water. And water varies from city to city. You probably don't want to buy a house where you hate the water.

I stand in the shower, because my sister lives in a house where the shower nozzle is at chin level. When I have to take a shower there, I have to do a back bend to get the shampoo out of my hair. Which reminds me of another thing: check the water pressure. There's nothing worse than taking a shower when the water drip-drip-drips out.

*Think about your household chores.* What work will need to be done routinely around the house? Where will you do laundry? Where will you put the groceries when you come in? Where will you put mops, brooms, vacuum cleaner?

*Imagine your furniture in this house.* Do you prefer this home with your old furniture or your old home with new furniture? You may dislike your current home for reasons you don't realize.

## If You Don't Like Something, Can You Change It?

Keep in mind that certain aspects of the house are unchangeable. You can't move the garage to the other side of the house. You can't change the house's location. (Well, I suppose you can if you want to go to the trouble of moving the house, but it's not likely.) You can't change the shape of the attic.

Other things are changeable. If you don't like the carpeting, for instance, you can have it replaced. Wallpaper, paint, curtains can all be changed. Sometimes when you're looking at a home, you have to look past the decorating to see the actual home underneath. When you're redoing the house in your imagination, keep in mind the cost of any redecorating or remodeling. Sure, you can redo the kitchen so that it has just the layout, cabinets, and flooring you want, but at what price?

**No Problem**

If you find yourself in love with a house that has a shower head positioned for a munchkin, you can always install a shower head on a hose (takes about 15 minutes). If you're really ambitious, you can even raise the position of the pipe.

# Is the House Well Maintained?

You love the house. It has charm, character, and all the features you could want. Are you ready to make an offer? Better wait. Behind that beautiful facade could be a cracking, leaking, stinking mess.

# Checking Out the Structure

When you look at the house, you should consider its structure — the exterior, electricity, plumbing, and so on. Here are some points to consider:

*Check the exterior of the home to see that it's well maintained.* Do you see peeling paint? Missing shingles? What will you need to do to maintain the house?

*Check the roof.* An inspector will check the roof more carefully, but you may be able to spot problems right away. Moss on the roof usually indicates moisture. Cracked, curled, or missing shingles may indicate that the roof needs repair. If it's winter and all the other houses have snow on the roof and yours doesn't, the house may be poorly insulated.

*Check the gutters* to be sure they're intact and attached.

*Check the electricity.* Again, an inspector will carefully check the electrical wiring, but you can make sure there are outlets placed conveniently in all the rooms. Also determine the monthly electric bill. You can usually get this information from the agent or directly from the electric company with just the address of the house.

*Check the interior walls and ceilings.* Are they drywall? Plaster? Are the interior walls in good shape? Any cracks? Keep in mind that some cracks will appear as a normal result of the house settling — it doesn't mean the house is going to fall in, but your inspector should take a close look at structure.

*Check the condition of flooring.* Is the carpet in good shape? Are the floors level? Is the tile or linoleum cracked or dirty? Do the floors creak? There are remedies for these problems, but it's best to know about them ahead of time.

*Check the basement.* Is it dry? Any indication of water damage? If the home owners store a lot of stuff on the basement floor, it probably means it's dry.

*Check the insulation.* Check the attic to see if the home is properly insulated. Make sure the storm windows are in good shape. Are they broken or bent?

**Power Watch**

If you see a tangle of extension cords in a room, it probably means that the room doesn't have adequate wall outlets.

Check the local utilities. Is trash collection included as part of the taxes? Do you use city water and city sewers? If so, what's the fee?

*Check the heating.* How is the house heated? Is it air-conditioned? If so, how — central air or window units? Is the air-conditioning sufficient? What's the monthly heating bill?

## Is the Neighborhood Acceptable?

Chapter 6 explained how to pinpoint a neighborhood that you like, then find a house. Here you're doing the opposite — finding the house and then double-checking the neighborhood. Of course, if you're only looking for houses in neighborhoods you've already checked out, then you're in good shape. You can skip this step.

## How Much Are the Taxes?

Your agent or the home owners should provide you with the general taxes for the area. They'll be included on the listing sheet.

The taxes will affect your monthly payments. The lender will also consider the taxes in determining what you can afford to pay each month.

Find out when taxes are reassessed. In some places, taxes are reassessed every few years. If you're due for a reassessment, the taxes may be raised. In other places, taxes are reassessed when a property is sold. In this case, you might have to come up with more money for the closing as well as for the taxes. Ask your agent.

## Your House and the 'Hood

Take a look at your house and the surrounding neighborhood. Does it fit in? A modest house in a more expensive area has the highest resale value. The most expensive house in a modest area has the lowest resale value.

## Checking the Area

Even if you find your dream home, you aren't going to be happy if your next-door neighbors have a garage band called Ear Drum Explosions who practice every night. You should take a close look at your neighbors, your neighborhood, and your community. Here are some avenues to explore:

*Drive around the immediate area.* Do you notice any bad neighbors? Loud dogs? Unsightly homes? Man-eating tigers? Are there a lot of rental properties? You will have to define for yourself the type of neighborhood you'll be comfortable with. Once when we were looking at a house, the next-door neighbor came over and told us how his brother, who also lived there, was arrested the night before for beating his wife. Not my idea of someone I'd borrow a cup of sugar from.

*Consider your routine.* Where will you shop? How far do you have to drive to get a six-pack of Cokes? How far is it to your office? What's the traffic like?

*Drive around the city.* What's the downtown like? Are the businesses well kept or is it a ghost town? Are the people friendly?

**Insurance Valves**

Property insurance is cheaper if your property is close to a fire hydrant, you have a burglar alarm system, or you live in a newer home.

## What Are the Schools Like?

Investigating the school district will be important if you have children. Even if you don't have children, living in a good district can increase the resale value of your home. Here are some strategies for making sure the schools make the grade:

*Figure out which school district you're in and which schools are available.* Are there private as well as public schools in the area? Find out how the children get to school. Do they walk? Ride a bus?

*Visit the schools.* Examine curriculum, class load, school policies. Talk to the principal. Talk to the teachers. Do they welcome your visit? Are they open?

*Ask a lot of questions.* What is the average class size? How do students rate on the standardized tests? How many students graduate? How many go on to college? What is the per-pupil expenditure? What extracurricular activities are supported?

*Talk to other parents in the area.* How involved are they? What do the parents like and dislike about the school? What is the general reputation of the school? You might want to attend a parent-teacher meeting, if possible.

## What About Emergencies?

You may not want to live right next door to a hospital unless you like the sounds of screaming sirens, but you should know where the closest medical facility is and make sure it's up to your standards.

You should also find out where the nearest fire and police stations are. What's the crime rate in the area? You can check with the local police station for crime statistics, or you might check out the Police Blotter section of the local paper, which can tell you more about the types of crimes — vandalism, public intoxication, versus burglary or assault.

## What About Fun?

In addition to looking into the public services provided in a community, check the recreational facilities. Think about what you like to do and then be sure you'll have the means to do it. Does the community have a local library? Is there a swimming pool nearby? Golf courses? Tennis courts? Does the area have well-kept parks? Are the facilities easy to get to? Are they overcrowded?

## The Least You Need to Know

Finding a house you like involves 20% research and 80% gut instinct. As you're looking, keep these points in mind:

➤ Your agent will set up appointments for you to tour different homes and will accompany you on the tour. You should ask your agent a lot of questions; after all, she's the expert. Ask her opinion of the home.

➤ When you tour the home, ask yourself these questions: Do you like the house? Does the house meet your needs? Can you live in the house?

➤ Keep in mind that some things can't be changed, and some things can. For example, don't rule out a house just because you hate the wallpaper.

➤ You should have the house thoroughly inspected by a professional, but as you tour the home, be sure to look at the structure — plumbing, wiring, heating, exterior, interior, and so on.

➤ Get information about the taxes on the home, the school district, the neighborhood, and community services.

# Part II
# Make an Offer

*After you find your dream house, you have to negotiate to buy it. Doing so can be pretty tense. What's a good price to offer? Will the sellers take your offer? Will you have to counteroffer? Your agent can help you with the negotiations. If all goes well, at the end of the process, you'll own a home!*

# Chapter 8

# Making an Offer

**In this chapter**

➤ Understanding the sales contract
➤ Deciding on a price
➤ Deciding on terms
➤ Making a deposit

I hate negotiating for anything. But others love the game. To these people, bargaining is part of the fun. If you like negotiation, you'll like the process of making an offer on a home. If you don't like to negotiate, don't worry. That's what agents are for. This chapter covers the art of making an offer.

## Understanding the Sales or Purchase Contract

When you've found the house you want, you make a formal offer on the house. Real estate laws differ from place to place. What the contract looks like and what it includes will vary. This section gives an overview of what's included in the offer; later sections explain the components of an offer in more detail. This section also includes some tips on making a successful offer.

## What's Included in the Offer

Your agent should help you decide what to include in the offer and then help you write it. Usually, the agent will use a preprinted offer form, modified to match what you want to offer. All offers should be submitted in written form and should include the following:

➤ The address and legal description of the property.

➤ The names of the brokers involved.

➤ The price, down payment, loan amount, and the amount of the deposit. Deciding on the price to offer is covered in "How Much Do You Offer?" later in this chapter.

➤ A time limit for the response to the offer, getting financing, closing on the house, and moving in.

➤ Certain conditions that must be met. For example, the offer will probably be contingent on your ability to obtain financing. Contingencies are covered in "What Terms?"

There may be other provisions, such as the inclusion of personal property, prorated payments, the handling of assumptions, damages, and other special circumstances.

## Tips on Making an Offer

When you're working up an offer, consider that all offers are a combination of price and terms. If you give something on price, you can expect to take something on terms. For instance, you might offer close to the selling price, but ask for a shorter closing or other terms. Or if the roof needs to be replaced, you could tell the seller to fix the roof or lower the price in exchange for fixing the roof yourself. Any obvious repairs should be addressed in the initial offer.

When you make an offer on a house, everything is negotiable — the price, the terms, the occupancy date, the personal property that's included, everything. You should ask for what you want. You may not get it, but you can ask. Unless you're in a very competitive seller's market, don't offer your best price first. Leave room for negotiating.

In the contract, be specific and include everything in writing. You may have a verbal agreement that the washer and dryer remain, but without a written contract, you'll have no recourse if the seller takes the washer and dryer anyway. Being specific is especially important when it comes to personal property, because what you consider personal property and what the seller considers personal property may differ. When in doubt, put it in writing.

The more contingencies you include in the offer, the less attractive the offer will be to the seller. That's okay if you're in a buyer's market. In a seller's market, though, if you really want the house, consider making an offer close to or at the asking price, and omit any contingencies.

Keep in mind that the contract will become a legal document if it's accepted. Consider having a lawyer look over the contract before you submit it.

# How Much Do You Offer?

When buying a home, you're bartering. You have to decide how much to pay for the home. Do you offer less than the listing price? If so, how much less? Do you offer the exact listing price? Or do you offer more than the listing price? In deciding on how much to offer, you need to consider the selling prices of comparable homes, the motivation of the seller, the price you can afford to pay, and how motivated you are to buy.

## Comparing Other Selling Prices

You don't want to pay more for the home than it's worth, but how can you figure out what a particular home is worth? One way is to ask your agent. Your agent has lots of experience in selling homes, so he should be able to give you his opinion of a fair price.

Another strategy is to find out the selling price of comparable homes in the area. Your agent can get these figures for you. Ask for statistics of list price versus selling price. As you look at several homes, you'll know what the home is listed for, and you can compare the home you want to these other listings. What a home lists for and what it sells for can be quite different. Ask your agent to investigate the selling prices of comparable homes. If similar homes in the area sold for $100,000, and the listing price of the home you want is $120,000, you

## Who's in Charge?

Strictly speaking, your agent usually works for the seller, unless you've made an agreement that the agent works exclusively for you. She probably wouldn't (or shouldn't) give you an inaccurate price to offer, but remember she's motivated to make the sale.

may want to offer less. Most homes sell for about 6% less than list price, but that's just an average. The actual difference varies depending on the location and the current market.

Another way to determine the market value of a home is to have it appraised before you make an offer. The house will be appraised for the lender in any case if you're applying for a mortgage, but this appraisal occurs after you've signed the deal. In the meantime, if you have the house appraised, and if you make your offer contingent upon the appraisal, you may be able to negotiate a lower price. See the section "What Terms?" later in this chapter. If you pay for an appraisal and the sellers sell the home to someone else, though, you'll have lost the appraisal fee.

# How Motivated Is the Seller?

When you're deciding on a fair price, you should also consider the mindset of the sellers. The sellers probably won't come right out and say they're desperate, but certain clues can give away the sellers' thinking. For instance, find out how long the house has been on the market. If the house was just put on the market, the sellers might not be too anxious to take the first offer. If the house has been on the market for several months, the seller may be more ready to accept an offer.

## Don't Be Misled

If the agent leads you to homes way out of your range, you should probably get another agent.

Find out whether the price has been reduced and, if so, how many times. A house that has been reduced several times may be ripe for an offer. Ask your agent to tell you when the sellers originally bought the house, what they paid for it, and how much equity they've accumulated.

A buyer's agent may be able to ferret out other information from the listing agent. For instance, are the sellers being transferred? Is the couple divorcing? Have they had other offers?

# Can You Afford the House?

You may think that this is the first question you should ask when you're considering a house. Certainly, being able to afford a house is a critical part of deciding what to offer — even in deciding whether to make an offer.

Your agent will probably keep you focused on homes in your price range, so you shouldn't have to fret too much about whether you can afford the home. If you find yourself looking at houses slightly out of your range, you may decide you can — somehow — spend a little more. For example, suppose that you feel you can afford a $150,000 house, but find the perfect house for $160,000. You may find a way to come up with a little more money. Perhaps you can sell off some assets. Or you can consider a different type of financing that will enable you to qualify for a larger loan.

# What Terms?

In addition to including the price of the house, you should also specify the terms of the sale. The terms can include any of the following:

*What else you want the seller to provide.* For instance, you may ask the seller to help pay for the closing costs or provide a warranty.

*What else has to happen for the deal to go through (in other words, contingencies).* For example, you may want to make the offer contingent upon getting financing.

*A deadline for response, settlement, and occupancy.* For example, you may give the seller two days to respond to the offer. You may ask for 60 days to secure financing and then require the seller to be out of the house on the day of the closing. The custom varies depending on the area.

*What else is included with the house,* such as appliances, window treatments, Porsche in the garage (you wish!).

*The required condition of the house at settlement.* For example, you may want to request that certain repairs be made.

*Other provisions,* such as the proration of taxes, club dues, and so on.

# What Else from the Seller?

Keep in mind that everything is negotiable. You can ask the seller to do or include anything you want. For example, you may ask the seller to pay for some or all allowable closing costs, such as the inspection, title search, and survey.

In addition to monetary requests, you can ask the seller to make changes to the house. For instance, you may ask the seller to have the roof repaired or to replace the carpeting (or allow for a redecorating fee).

# Contingencies

Suppose you agree to purchase a house, but can't get a loan. Or suppose you agree to purchase a house, but find out in the meantime that the house is riddled with termites. If you didn't include any contingency clauses in your contract, you'd be stuck with buying the house anyway. A contingency clause says "Sure, I'll buy this house, if…."

This section covers some common contingencies that are included in sales agreements.

# Financing

If you can't get financing for the home, you will have to bow out of the deal. You should also specify exactly what financing is acceptable. For instance, you could get a loan from Eddie the Armbreaker at 20% interest, but would you want to?

You should specifically state the following:

➤ The amount of time you have to get financing
➤ The loan amount
➤ The down payment amount
➤ The maximum interest rate you'll pay
➤ The type and term of loan

## The Deed and Title

You will want a clear deed and title to the house. Usually the buyer pays for the title search, but the contract should specify what happens if problems arise.

## The Inspection

You may want to make the sale conditional on a professional inspection of the home. (Inspections are covered in Chapter 14.) You should specify who pays for the inspection and what happens if the inspector finds a problem. For example, just having the sale contingent on an inspection doesn't ensure that the seller has to fix the broken toilet. Is the seller required to fix a problem? All problems? Can you withdraw the offer if the inspection isn't acceptable? You should work out these terms with your agent.

You may also want to have the house inspected for termites, radon, lead paint, asbestos, old hockey players, or other hazards. Your lender may require some of these tests before approving the loan.

## The Appraisal

Your lender will require an appraisal of the property before the loan is approved. You can make your offer contingent on an appraisal, and you can spell out what to do if the appraisal comes back lower than the selling price. Can you renegotiate the price? Can you withdraw from the deal?

## Other Contingencies

If you already own a home, you can make your purchase contingent upon selling it. In fact, some lenders make financing contingent upon the sale of your home.

Sometimes a contingency is countered with an escape clause, or kickout. For example, the seller may want to continue to show the house. If the seller receives another offer, you'll have the option of removing the contingency or backing out.

Keep in mind that the more contingencies, the less attractive the offer. Also, it's usually not a good idea to include frivolous contingencies: "I won't buy the house unless the sellers paint it pink."

## Setting Time Limits

Buying a home is a waiting game. You should specify how long you'll wait. How long do the sellers have to respond to your offer? You should require a written response within a certain period — for instance, 48 hours. If you don't require a response, the seller can sit on your offer, perhaps until a better offer comes along. But remember, you can cancel an offer any time before it has been accepted.

How long until you close on the house? In setting this date, allow enough time for your loan application and approval.

You will likely move in immediately after closing. But you may make a special arrangement for the sellers to remain in the house after closing and pay you rent. If this is the case, the exact terms should be spelled out in the contract.

## Personal Property

Personal property is defined as anything that can be picked up and moved. Anything that's attached is real property. The sellers are entitled to take their personal property, but must leave the real property. Seems clear enough, until you move into your house and find that the sellers took the wall-to-wall carpeting, curtains, stove, refrigerator, dishwasher, cabinets, lightbulbs, and anything else that wasn't nailed down tight.

To avoid such a situation, you should explicitly identify items you want the sellers to leave. Do you want all the window treatments? Ceiling fans? What about the pot rack hanging in the kitchen? The chandelier in the dining room? What appliances are included? The washer, dryer, dishwasher, refrigerator, stove? What about any rugs? Mirrors? Stained glass?

If a certain possession is key to the house layout, you may ask for it to be included. For example, suppose that the kitchen includes a bar and stools for dining at the counter. You may ask the sellers to leave the stools; they may not need them in their new house anyway.

## Condition of House at Settlement

In the contract, state the condition in which you expect to receive the house. For instance, you may state that the plumbing, heating, mechanical and electrical systems are in working order at closing. You may want the house empty and "broom clean."

You should request a walk-through inspection right before closing to ensure that the house is in the same condition as it was when you made the offer. If you want a walk-through, put it in the offer. If you take one, check for any damage to the property — holes in the wall, broken windows, marks in the flooring, spots on the carpet. Check the heating, air-conditioning, plumbing, and other components to make sure they're working. See Chapter 15 for information on how to handle problems found at the walk-through.

## Prorations and Adjustments

The contract should identify items that will be prorated and how. For example, the sellers may have already paid taxes and utility bills on the house for the next three months. Are they entitled to a portion of the money back? Or taxes may be due, and you may want the sellers to pay a prorated amount. Depending on the type of loan and the situation, different items will be handled differently.

## Other Provisions

The contract may include other provisions such as confirmation of the type of zoning, explanation of what happens if the house burns down in the meantime, statement of what type of sewer and water, statement of assignability, and so on. Your agent should explain any other provisions included in the contract.

# Making a Deposit

When you make an offer on a house, the seller will want to know you're committed to making the purchase and will usually require a deposit. The amount varies, but should be specified in the contract. The contract should also state who holds the deposit until closing. (The real estate agent should put the money into a trust account. That's a special account in which money sits undisturbed and earning interest — which is yours — until a specified action takes place.)

# The Least You Need to Know

Making an offer on a house can be scary. You're making a big commitment — to living in a certain location, to making payments for a long time. Take your time and be sure you understand any offers you do make.

➤ The sales contract, once signed by both parties, is a legally binding contract. Your agent should help you prepare the contract. You may also want to have your lawyer look it over. In this case, have the lawyer look over the contract before you sign, or make the offer contingent upon a lawyer's approval within 24 hours of acceptance.

➤ Critical items to cover in the sales agreement include a description of the property, the price, financing terms, response time, settlement date, and any contingencies.

➤ You can decide on a fair price to offer by seeing what comparable homes have sold for in the area. Also take into consideration your motivation and the seller's motivation.

➤ Common contingencies include getting financing and having the home inspected.

➤ In the sales agreement, spell out any personal property you want included as part of the sale.

# Chapter 9

# Negotiating

## In this chapter

➤ Understanding the offer process

➤ Using an appropriate strategy

➤ Handling counteroffers

➤ Having an offer accepted

➤ Withdrawing from an offer

➤ Using a real estate lawyer

The tennis game begins when you make the first serve. The ball goes to the seller. The seller may decide not to play or may return the offer to you. If he returns the offer, the ball's back in your court. You may decide to quit, or you may return the offer. The ball goes back to the seller. This back and forth process, or *negotiation*, continues until a deal is made or someone quits.

Understanding the fine art of negotiating can help you make a good offer to begin with and then handle any counteroffers. This chapter discusses negotiating techniques.

# Understanding the Offer Process

When you decide you want to make an offer on a house, your agent will sit down with you and help you write it. The offer must be written; it cannot be verbal. (Chapter 8 explains the key items included in an offer.) After the offer is written, you sign it and attach your deposit to show the sellers, "Look. I want your house, and here's some money to prove it."

Your agent then conveys the offer to the seller, usually in a face-to-face meeting with the seller's agent. The offer may be made over the phone or faxed, then followed up with a face-to-face meeting. This is one area where your agent can help; she can present the offer favorably and start the negotiations.

When you write the offer, you should include a time limit for responding to it. During this period, you'll be biting your nails and sitting by the phone, until finally your agent will give you the seller's response: yes, no, or maybe.

The seller may choose to accept the offer, in which case you can skip to the section later in this chapter titled "Having an Offer Accepted." You've bought yourself a house.

Sometimes the seller chooses not to respond. In this case, no news is not good news. No news means no. If the seller rejects the offer and you really want the house, you may want to make another offer. Or you can start looking at other houses of interest.

In many cases, the seller will return the offer with some changes. This is called a *counteroffer*. You can choose to accept it and go directly to the section titled "Having an Offer Accepted," or you can choose to counter with your next offer. In this case, see the section "Handling Counteroffers." The back and forth of countering will continue until one side quits or one side accepts the deal.

**Don't Have a Cow, Man**

Buying a home is an emotional process. You may think that only one house will really fit you and your needs, and you may feel devastated if that deal doesn't go through. Keep in mind that there are many, many houses, and you'll most likely find another house that you like.

# Offer Strategies

Depending on your situation, you may want to use one of the following strategies:

*The lowball offer.* If you're looking for a house in a buyer's market and aren't emotionally committed to having the house, you may want to make a lowball offer. A lowball offer is usually way below the asking price. Lowballs may succeed if the seller is desperate. Sometimes the seller will counter, but most times the seller will feel insulted and ignore this type of offer. You definitely don't want to make a lowball offer in a seller's market or if you really, really want the house.

An agent must pass along any offer you make. He may not want to take a lowball offer to a seller, but he has to.

*The anxious offer.* If you feel you must have the house, you may want to make your best offer first. This strategy leaves no room for negotiating, but might be necessary in a seller's market in which homes aren't on the market for long. Your agent will probably convey to the sellers that this is your best offer; the sellers may accept, counter, or reject the offer. If the market isn't red hot, you may not want to make your best offer first. Most sellers expect to receive an offer, counter, then receive another offer; that is, they expect to play tennis.

*The bidding war offer.* In a seller's market, you may find yourself bidding with other buyers for the same property. In this case, you lose all your negotiating strength. You have to see the bid, raise it, or fold your cards gracefully and move to the next game.

## Win-Win Negotiating

A lot of people think that a successful deal happens only when they impose their will on another and get their way entirely (a win-lose situation). The best deals, though, are when both negotiating parties are happy (a win-win situation). If you buy a house at the price you want and the terms you want, and the sellers also get the price they want at acceptable terms, you both benefit.

*The negotiable offer.* In most cases, the best offer is the one that leaves room for negotiating. You should plan your first offer and your maximum offer. If you're working with a buyer's agent, your agent can help you with this strategy. If you're working with a seller's agent or subagent, keep in mind that this agent is required to pass along all information. If you tell the seller's agent you can go higher, the seller's agent can pass that information along. The negotiable offer gives you a start in the point-counterpoint process, described next.

# Handling Counteroffers

If the sellers want to consider your offer, but make some changes, they'll return a counteroffer. If you want to make some changes to the counteroffer, you make another counteroffer. And so it goes.

## Receiving a Counteroffer

If a seller counters with another offer, that's usually a good sign — at least you know that the seller gave your offer some consideration. Your agent should return the counteroffer and explain the changes. Usually, there's a time limit for you to respond to the counteroffer.

Keep in mind that everything is negotiable. The seller may ask for more, may say no to what you asked for, or may ask for something else. For instance, the seller may ask for a higher price. Or the seller may say no to your request to pay for a survey. The seller may agree to the offer but ask for a different closing date or occupancy date. You should look over the counteroffer carefully and be sure you understand the changes.

**Get It in Writing**

Don't accept or respond to any verbal counteroffers. If the sellers tell your agent that they want a higher price, get that information in the form of a written offer.

Items that remain the same are not mentioned again after they have been found okay — only changes are noted on counters. If you're not sure which things are the same and which are different, ask. You may want to restate your understanding in the counteroffer.

In some cases, the counteroffer may be okay with you. You sign the counteroffer, and the deal is made. See the section "Having an Offer Accepted," later in this chapter.

In other cases, you may think the counteroffer is close, but you still want a few changes. In this case, you counter the counteroffer with another counteroffer!

# Responding to a Counteroffer

If the seller's counteroffer is close to what you want, but you want to make a few changes, you can offer another counteroffer. Again, your agent will help you draw up the offer. Usually the counteroffer is simply an edited version of the original offer, with changes written and then initialed by all parties. In some cases, you may want to write a new offer.

In responding to the counteroffer, you should consider what's important to you. Can you come up a little higher on price? Will you give on price in exchange for something else?

When negotiating, be sure you stay within your financial limitations. Don't let the emotions of buying a house sway you into paying more than you can afford. It's easy to get into a nitpicking situation during countering. You may think that you want the last word. Keep in mind your goal: to buy the house. If you want to change something that's really important, by all means don't accept the counteroffer. If the reason you want to counter is trivial, consider just accepting the offer.

If you're close to a deal, the agent may recommend you split the difference. For example, if you offer $105,000, and the seller counters with $108,000, you may split the difference and offer $106,500. In this case, both sides may feel as if they won. But don't do this too soon.

The best type of negotiating is a win-win situation. The sellers should feel as if they got a good price, and the buyers should feel as if they got a good deal on the house they wanted.

## Keep it Clean

If you're making lots of changes, you may want to use a new offer form. If the sellers see many items crossed off or written in, they may be more aware of the changes. The marked-up form screams, "Here's where I'm trying to get you!" Instead, write up a new offer that looks cleaner. Be sure it says what you want it to say.

**No Deal**

An offer is accepted only when all parties have signed the same document. Don't be fooled if the seller or agent says, "The offer is accepted, with just a few changes." If the seller made any changes to an offer you presented, it's a rejected offer, and you're not bound to honor the agreement.

## When to Quit

If the counteroffering has become ridiculous — gone on for too long or become fixated on small details — it's time to quit. Sometimes the buyer and seller focus on the competitiveness of the situation and feel driven to win. The process can get ugly, and usually both the buyer and the seller end up with bad feelings.

Don't let the negotiations drag you down. Your agent can help keep you focused on the goal (buying the house). Your agent may also be able to get the sellers to focus on their goal (selling the house). If not, you should consider walking away and trying to find another house suited to your needs.

You may also want to quit when it becomes apparent that you and the seller are too far off on terms and price to reach an acceptable agreement.

## Having an Offer Accepted

The happy part of house hunting occurs when the offer is accepted. This occurs when the seller signs and accepts your original offer or any counteroffers, or when you sign and accept the seller's counteroffer. Once both parties have signed, the purchase offer becomes a legally binding document. You can't back out now.

When your offer is accepted, you'll probably feel two conflicting emotions: happy (you should be glad that you've purchased the house you wanted) and scared (you just made a big commitment, and the process isn't entirely over). You still have to get financing and close on the house. (Someone should make a pill to treat buyer's remorse!) Keep in mind that most people feel nervous after making such a big decision, and the feeling will probably pass.

When your offer is accepted, make sure you get a copy of the signed agreement. You may want to have a lawyer look over the agreement before you sign it. If your lawyer isn't available, you can write "Subject to the approval in form of my lawyer." See the section "Do I Need a Real Estate Lawyer?" later in this chapter.

You may be asked to increase the amount of money you put down on the home. This money will be held in trust until you close on the house.

You'll also have to get moving on any contingencies that you need to satisfy. For example, you may have a certain period (specified in the contract) in which to arrange to have the home inspected. You may also have to apply for a loan within a certain period. Your agent should remind you what you need to do next.

## Withdrawing an Offer

Suppose you change your mind and decide, "Oops — I don't really want to buy a house." Can you back out of a deal? In some cases, you can. In other cases, the seller is going to respond with, "Oops to you, bub — you're getting a house whether you want it or not!"

> **Mind Games**
>
> If you feel anxious about the house, make a list of all the things you like about it and all the benefits you'll enjoy from owning it. Start thinking about how you'll decorate, who you'll invite over, and so on. Think about living in the house and enjoying it. Doing so may help ease your mind.

When can you back out of a deal? You can withdraw from the deal with no legal repercussions in any of the following cases:

➤ You can withdraw an offer any time before the seller has signed and accepted it.

➤ You can walk away at any time during the offer-counteroffer process. If the seller gives you an offer you don't like, you don't have to respond. You can just quit.

➤ You can withdraw an offer if any of the contingencies included in the offer aren't met. If the offer is contingent on an inspection of the home, and the inspection turns up a major structural flaw, you may be able to withdraw from the offer. (Usually, though, the seller has the opportunity to make the repairs.)

If the offer has been signed by both parties, it's a binding contract. You can't back out without forfeiting your deposit. Also, the sellers may sue you for damages if you don't fulfill the contract. On the other hand, the seller can't back out either. If the seller does, you can sue for damages or try to enforce the contract. You can't really force people to buy or sell a house unless they want to, though.

# Do I Need a Real Estate Lawyer?

You may want to use a real estate lawyer to look over the contract before you sign it. A lawyer, for the most part, will not get involved in negotiating the deal, but can help ensure that you don't get caught up in a bad deal. The lawyer can look over the finer details of the agreement and make sure that you understand them and that they're acceptable.

A lawyer is necessary to help with the closing, conduct the title search, deal with your lender, ensure that all the necessary steps are completed, and look over any papers you have to sign. (You'll be signing a lot!)

She can also help settle any difficulties that arise. For instance, suppose the deal falls through because of one of the contingencies, but the sellers won't return the deposit. Your lawyer can help handle this problem.

You should use a lawyer who specializes in real estate law. You can ask friends, relatives, your agent, or others for recommendations. Be sure to inquire about the lawyer's fees. You may pay a flat fee or an hourly fee. Also, be sure you explain exactly what you want the lawyer to help with.

# The Least You Need to Know

If you like to negotiate, you'll enjoy the strategies of the home-buying process. If you hate negotiating, you can rely on your agent to keep your nerves calm and help you through the offer-counteroffer stages of the negotiation.

➤ When you make an offer on a house, the sellers can accept, decline, or counter with their own offer. If you receive a counteroffer, you can then accept, decline, or counter with your next offer. This process continues until a deal is made or someone quits.

➤ When both parties agree to the offer and sign it, it becomes a legally binding contract. Once you have a binding contract, you can't withdraw from the offer without legal consequences.

➤ You can withdraw from the offer before the seller signs or any time during the offer-counteroffer process. If the contingencies you specified in your contract aren't met, you may also be able to withdraw your offer.

➤ If you start to quibble about minor things and the process gets ugly, you may consider quitting and moving on to another house. You may also want to quit if it becomes apparent that you and the seller are too far apart on terms and/or price.

**If at first you don't succeed, find out if the loser gets anything.**

—Bill Lyon

# Buying a New Home

Thousands of new homes are sold each year. Perhaps you are one of the thousands who want a brand-new home in a brand-new neighborhood with brand-new carpeting, brand-new appliances, brand-new everything. There's something thrilling about newness.

Buying a new home and buying an existing home are similar in some aspects. The process of finding a home, making an offer, getting financing, and closing are basically the same. But there are some variations in finding a good home and in making a good offer, as covered in this chapter.

Chapter 5 discusses the pros and cons of buying a new home compared to buying an existing home.

# Finding a House

Finding a newly built house is in some ways similar to finding an existing house. First, you should select a good location and a house plan that meets your needs. Then you should find a high-quality home. When you look at existing homes, you can see what you're getting. When you buy a new home — especially if it hasn't been built yet — you have only a drawing on paper and the builder's word that the home you see is the home you'll get. You can't do much about the drawing, but you should investigate the builder. This section explains all the items to consider in finding a new house.

# Selecting a Subdivision

Finding a new home may be easier or harder than finding an existing home, depending on how you look at it. On the plus side, most new homes are built in new subdivisions. The developers and builders most likely advertise these new developments in the real estate section of the paper. You may also spot subdivisions as you drive around the city.

On the minus side, most new subdivisions are located outside the city, where there's room to expand. In this case, you may have to look a little harder to find a subdivision that's in an area acceptable to you. As you look at the subdivision, take into consideration the following questions:

*Is the subdivision close to the place where you work?* Is the commuting time acceptable? Do you have access to a highway?

*Is the area around the subdivision acceptable?* If the subdivision is within an existing neighborhood, you can check out the neighborhood. If the subdivision is surrounded by vacant land, you can investigate the plans for the area. For instance, you probably shouldn't move into a subdivision if the rest of the surrounding area is planned for commercial development.

*What's the growth rate in that area of the city?* No matter how wonderful the subdivision, you won't want to live in an area of town that's on the skids. Think about reselling the house. Will you be able to do so at a profit? Or are sales in the area flat? Are they on a downswing?

*Is shopping convenient?* Are there enough cultural and recreational facilities in the area to meet your needs? What's planned for the community?

*What are the local schools like?* Even if you don't have children, you should consider the school system. Living in a good district can improve the resale value of your home.

*What police and fire services will be provided in the new subdivision?*

*What will the taxes be?* Will you have to pay for any special assessments to install sewer lines, for instance, or sidewalks? Are taxes applied differently to resale homes and new homes? Will the quality of home in the subdivision be consistent? How many homes have been sold in the subdivision?

# Selecting a Good Builder

When you think about selecting a house, think about the three little pigs. You don't want a house that a huff and a puff will blow over. The quality of the home depends a lot on the builder.

Many subdivisions include houses built by different builders. You should tour several homes in the subdivision to see which homes you like. Try to focus on the quality of the home, not the "Wow!" factor or the price.

Investigate the sales of homes in the subdivision. Which are the best-selling homes? Why? Are they better built? Better priced?

If you have friends in the home construction or home maintenance industries, ask them for their thoughts. They may know that houses built by SlapEmUp Homes are a nightmare. They can also tell you which builders have the worst and best reputations. Your real estate lawyer can help, too.

Ask the builder reps why one house is better than another. Of course, they're going to give you a sales pitch, but ask for concrete details. Does one builder use better roofing materials? Does one builder include other extras as part of the deal (for instance, landscaping)?

Determine the basics and extras for a given home. Find out the costs for upgrading. For example, if one builder offers more extras in a home or charges less for upgrades, you should consider that builder.

Visit other homes built by the builder and talk to home owners. These owners may be able to tell you about any problems they've had. You may also want to visit a more established subdivision where the builder has built homes. These home owners can tell you how the

### Beauty is Skin Deep

Keep in mind that a model home has top-quality carpet, cabinets, tiles, appliances, and so on. Your home may not include the same features. If you're touring the model home, be sure to ask whether you'll get the exact carpet, exact tile, and so on. If not, check the quality of the materials that will be used in your home. If you want to upgrade, inquire about the costs.

houses have stood up in the long term. Ask the home owners what they like and what they dislike. Which builders have good resale track records? Do their homes appreciate, do they sell quickly once placed on the market, or is there something that keeps buyers away?

Check the reputation of the builder. How long has the builder been constructing new homes? Is the builder solidly financed? Check with the Better Business Bureau and other consumer groups to see whether any complaints have been made against the builder. In some provinces, reputable builders register with the housing ministry's warranty program. If your province operates such a program, contact the office and inquire about the builder of the home you're looking at.

## Selecting a Plan

After you decide on a particular builder, you can focus on selecting the home you want. Many builders offer several styles of home. The homes may also vary in size, amenities, and other aspects. You should tour several homes and see which one you prefer.

When you look at the house plans, think about you and your family's needs now and five years from now. Consider the following questions:

➤ How many bedrooms do you need? How many bathrooms? How large are the rooms?

➤ Where will your family work and play in the home: living room, den, dining room, and so on? Do you like the placement of the rooms in the house, the traffic pattern?

➤ What type of kitchen does the plan include? An eat-in kitchen? A country kitchen? What items in the kitchen can you select: appliances? Tile? Cabinets? What do you have to pay extra for?

➤ How big is the yard? Is landscaping included?

➤ Is a garage standard? Is it finished or unfinished?

➤ Does the house have a basement? How much will it cost for a full basement? Half basement? Finished? Unfinished?

➤ How is the house heated? Does it use the most energy-efficient heating source? What about central air? Central vacuum? Insulation?

➤ Which decorating options can you select? Can you pick the floor coverings? Wall coverings? Window treatments? If so, compare the quality and selection of each of these options. Do you have to pay more to upgrade the carpet or other interior elements?

**Finished, Almost**

The closer to completion, the more precisely you can determine what you're getting and the less chance of lengthy delays. Delays can be costly, especially if you have to sell your current home or terminate your lease.

➤ What's included in the sale, and what's extra? For instance, is a fence included or do you have to pay extra for it? Is the patio or deck included? How big is the standard patio and deck? Can you get a bigger one? For what price?

## Selecting a Good Lot

You've got your house and neighborhood. Now you have to plunk it down somewhere in that neighborhood. Where? You may be able to select any location in the subdivision you want. The best lot isn't the largest lot; it's the one with a view. Keep in mind that you may have to pay more for the house, depending on the lot you select. In some cases, you may not have a wide selection for the placement of the home. The builder may have only a few lots left.

When you select a lot, be sure to consider the traffic pattern in the neighborhood. Does everyone in that neighborhood have to drive by your house to

**To Tree or Not to Tree** WHOA!

Your house may overlook a beautiful row of trees when you move in, but that doesn't mean the builder won't rip out those trees to prepare another building lot. If the trees aren't actually on your own lot, you should ask the builder if they're there to stay.

get home? Will the street be busy? Does the house back onto a main road? Consider your view. Does the house back up to trees? Is your lot next to a school yard or church?

# Negotiating a Sales Contract

When you talk to a builder, you may get the impression that nothing is negotiable: the price is fixed. In some cases, the builder will hold firm to the price. That's because the builder has fixed costs that can't be avoided. The lumber is going to cost so much, the electrical work is going to cost so much, and so on. Most builders operate on a slim margin, so they don't usually give you much of a break on the price. But there's still some room for negotiation.

## Negotiating for Upgrades

Remember: what you see in the model home and what you get are different. The carpeting, wall covering, cabinets, tile, fixtures, etc., used in your home may vary, but for a price, you can upgrade to the better stuff. Here's where you can negotiate. Consider asking for any of the following improvements:

*Better-quality outside materials* (roofing and exterior walls).

*Landscaping.* In some cases, the covenants, conditions, and restrictions of the area may require a certain type of front yard. In such a case, the landscaping may be included as part of the price. If it's not, you may want to ask for landscaping.

*Better-quality floor and wall coverings* (carpet, tile, wallpaper, and so on).

*Better-quality appliances.* Identify the appliances that are included as part of the deal. The model home may include a dishwasher, but does yours? You may ask the builder to throw in some freebies.

**Save the Trees**

Usually a builder will clear an entire area of trees before he starts building. If you find a lot that still has mature trees on it, though, you should ask the builder to leave them. If the builder says no, and it's important to you, try negotiating. Offer to give up another perk in exchange for the trees.

*More or better amenities.* Is the fireplace extra? How about a free one? Is the deck included? How about a free hot tub?

You may not get all that you ask for, but you can still ask.

## Negotiating Contract Terms

Another area for negotiation includes the terms of the contract. For example, you might ask the builder to buy down the mortgage. (See Chapter 12 for information on this type of financing.) Or you can ask the builder to provide help with the closing costs. You may ask to do some of the work yourself in exchange for a break on price or features. Your agent can help you negotiate a favorable contract — which brings up a good question: should you use an agent?

## Using an Agent

As you look through a new house, the builder's rep may try to convince you that you don't need an agent. He may tell you, "You can buy directly from me and avoid the middleman!"

Be careful! Sometimes you need the middleman. For instance, if you have to negotiate face-to-face with the builder, you may lose your negotiating power. An experienced agent knows where you can push for a deal. Plus, the agent is an impartial negotiator. If you go to the builder with that "please-please-please-I-want-this-house" look on your face, you lose. It's difficult not to be emotional.

Also, the builder's rep is actually a commissioned agent, hired by the builder to sell the properties in the development. The rep will likely get the commission on the house himself anyway.

The builder cannot refuse to work with your agent and should pay the agent's commission. You pay the same price regardless of whether you use an agent. In many cases, in fact, a builder prefers to deal with buyers' agents

**Shop for Dough**

The builder may sell you on one-stop shopping — buy the house and arrange for the financing. That's okay as long as you're getting a competitive loan package. Shop around.

because they know they represent serious and qualified buyers.

Be sure to have a lawyer look over all the contracts before you sign.

## Getting a Deal

Builders are motivated to sell. They don't hold any emotional ties to the home. The builder's motivation determines the flexibility in sales terms. In some instances, you may be able to negotiate a better deal. Here are some examples:

*Buy early in the development process.* Once people start to live in the new homes in a subdivision, the area becomes more appealing to other buyers. The builder can say that he has already sold some homes and they're moving briskly, so that potential buyers will think they'd better buy now or be locked out of the neighborhood forever. So in the early stages of development, builders may be more flexible in negotiating. Some builders offer lower prices to the first five buyers, for example.

*Negotiate to buy the model.* The model will include top-quality furnishings, plus you can see exactly what you're getting. You may arrange for the builder to sell you the model and then let him rent the home from you until the development is complete.

*If you can, buy in a down market.* If new home sales are slow, the builder may want to unload the excess units. If he doesn't, he has to pay the costs to maintain and promote the sale of these empty units. Also, he has sunk a great deal of money into supplies and labor (he has to pay the subcontractors whether the house sells or not), so a builder in a bind may be willing to sell a house to recover his investment, just so he can pay off his bills.

*Buy the last unit.* As more and more homes in the subdivision sell, the builder gets more and more profit. He may be less worried about meeting expenses and may be flexible on price. Plus the builder is likely to want to move on to the next development and may be motivated to sell the last one.

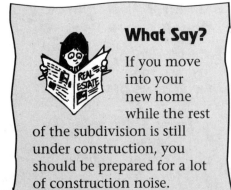

**What Say?**

If you move into your new home while the rest of the subdivision is still under construction, you should be prepared for a lot of construction noise.

# Home Warranties

What's a new home warranty? Do you need one? What types are there? What should the warranty include? Read on for the answers to these and other warranty questions.

## What's a Warranty?

A warranty is a guarantee that a product will function for a certain period. For example, your toaster may come with a 30-day warranty.

If the toaster doesn't work, you can get a new toaster or have it repaired. Home warranties work the same way.

## The Real McCoy

In most provinces, new home warranty programs are voluntary. But you should think twice about dealing with builders who don't voluntarily belong. (The New Home Warranty Plan is compulsory in Ontario.) Voluntary or not, the program covers a potential purchaser's deposit on a new home (usually up to $20,000) and defects in workmanship, to a maximum cost of $20,000.

### Sorry

New home warranty programs do not cover the purchase of a new condominium unit to the same extent as the purchase of a new home. Nor do they cover conversions of office buildings into condominiums. Check the fine print. Better still, get a lawyer's advice.

### Cover Yourself

A resale home warranty plan, which can also cover new homes, covers for one year the cost of repairs that are required, under normal operating conditions, to specific components of the house, such as the mechanical systems and major appliances. Coverage costs about $350, with $50 deductible for a service call, and can be purchased through a real estate agent, either by the vendor, to facilitate sale of the home, or the purchaser.

Some defects such as loose-fitting windows and doors are covered for one year; others, such as electrical and plumbing defects, are covered for two years; still others, such as fundamental problems with construction, are covered for seven years, depending on the province where you live.

In Ontario, you can obtain a booklet called *Home Buyer's Guide to After Sales Service*, published by the Ontario New Home Warranty Program. You can also get details about the program over the Internet, at *www.newhome.on.ca*.

# Avoiding Problems

Buying a new home shouldn't involve any more or any fewer hassles than buying an existing home. But you'll encounter a different set of problems. You may want to include the following information in your sales contract:

➤ You should insist on a final walk-through inspection before you close the deal. Insist that the builder fix any incomplete, missing, or broken items. If possible, don't close until the changes are made. If the builder resists, report him to the provincial housing authorities.

➤ Make sure that no money changes hands until the repairs are done. If the builder is paid, he may not be motivated to fix the dripping sink. If the money is still held in trust until he fixes that dripping tap, you then have some leverage to ensure that the builder makes the repairs.

➤ Make sure that your home is built to the standards of the model you visited. In some cases — for instance, if the housing market collapses — the builder may make changes.

➤ Ask for ongoing inspections. If you know someone with home-building experience, have him check out the house during its building phases. It's easier to spot shoddy electrical work — and have it fixed — when the work is being done.

➤ Prepare for delays. The builder may take longer to build the house than planned. This can cause problems if you don't have anywhere to live or if you've locked in the interest rate on your mortgage. First, make sure you have someplace to stay if the house isn't built on time. Second, consider locking in the rate until the closing date. You may ask for this if you're using the builder or mortgage company for financing. Third, check up on the progress. If four months have gone by since you made an offer and the builder hasn't started the basement yet, you're in trouble.

# What Are Your Rights?

The law gives a builder considerable flexibility in extending deadlines to complete construction. This allows a builder to presell most of the units in a development before he proceeds. The law applies differently to new houses and new condominiums, and gives a builder up to 18 months of additional time to finish a project.

If you buy a new home, you should not sell your current home or terminate your lease until you know with some certainty the date of your new home's completion.

If you think the delay is unconscionable, you have several options:

1. Talk to the builder. Since builders often develop several projects at once, you might offer to buy a finished home in another of the builder's projects.

2. Talk to your lawyer. Your lawyer can advise you on the remedy, if any, you can pursue.

3. Read the fine print in your contract with the builder. You'll usually find that the builder has more time than you'd have expected to complete the project.

# The Least You Need to Know

Buying a new house can be exciting because you can choose many of the details of the home — the floor plan, the carpet, the cabinets, and so on. When you purchase a new home, you don't want to get carried away in this excitement. You want to negotiate a good deal.

➤ The key items to consider when purchasing a new home are the area, builder, plot, and plan.

➤ Check out the builder's reputation. Talk to home owners already living in houses built by the same builder. Check with the Better Business Bureau. Ask those acquainted with home builders for their opinions. Check your builder's reputation with your real estate lawyer.

➤ New builders may not be too flexible on price, but you can negotiate for upgrades to the carpeting, roof, yard, etc. You can also negotiate on the terms of the contract.

➤ If you're having the home built (rather than buying a newly built home), expect delays.

➤ There are three types of new home warranties: an implied warranty, a builder's warranty, and an insurance-backed warranty. You should get all three.

# Buying a Condominium or Co-op

Hate to do lawn work? Want to live someplace where someone else cuts the grass and takes care of maintenance, but you still own your own place? If so, you may want to buy a different kind of home — a condominium, co-operative, or townhouse. This chapter explains each of these types of residences and suggests how you can make a smart purchase if you decide that this style of living is for you.

## Buying a Condominium

Take this little quiz:

True or False?    The term *condominium* refers to an apartment-style building where the tenants own the apartment.

**False**    Condominium actually refers not to the style of the house, but to the form of ownership. Also, condominiums come in many shapes and sizes. A condominium may be an apartment-style building, a duplex, a townhouse, or a freestanding home.

**True or False?** When you own a condominium, you don't actually own anything physical. You own airspace.

**Basically, true** When you purchase a condominium, you own the airspace inside the walls and a portion of the shared or common elements — for instance, sidewalks, pool, elevator, and so on. You don't own the walls or the ceilings of your residence. You own what's inside the walls and ceilings.

What are the benefits, then, of purchasing this type of residence? What are the drawbacks? The next section will help you decide whether condo living is right for you.

# Advantages and Disadvantages of Condominium Living

There are many reasons why a condominium might make sense for you: unlike an apartment that you rent, a condominium enables you to **build equity** during the time you live in it. You can also resell the condo. It's yours.

**Don't Forget the Fees**

Be sure to include the monthly fees for a condominium in calculating the monthly payments. In addition to PITI (payment, interest, taxes, insurance), you have to pay a monthly maintenance fee.

You have **less maintenance** to worry about, because the condominium association takes care of exterior repair and maintenance work. (Maintenance of your own unit, of course, is still up to you.) Your condominium may include **recreational facilities**: a swimming pool, tennis courts, recreation room, and more.

If you want to live in a certain area or neighborhood, a condominium may be your only option. For instance, in large cities such as Toronto you may find a better selection of condos than single-family homes in certain areas. In some cases, you may pay less for a condo than for a single-family home.

What are the drawbacks? In a slow market, condo prices usually suffer more than house prices and rebound later. If you have to sell during a downtime, you may not get the price you want, and it may take longer to sell the place. Also, as a member of a condo community, you must abide by the community's rules. The board, for instance, determines the improvements you can make to the facility, and you have to pitch in financially, whether you agree or not.

You may have less space and less privacy in a condo than in a single-family dwelling. In many developments, your neighbors are just a wall away. Neighbors can affect the resale value of a condo even more than they can a house. People are going to be choosier about the neighbor behind the wall than the neighbor across the backyard fence.

**Welcome Aboard**

Become a board member of the condo association. Doing so enables you to keep up on what's going on in your community, plus you have a say in decisions.

## The Board Rules!

Once a condominium development is completed and the owners or occupants move in, the owners set up a condo association, which then elects a board of directors. As a member of the condominium community, you can vote for board members and express your views on other issues. You can — and probably should — run for the board yourself. The number of votes you control often depends the size, location, view, or floor plan of your condominium. Larger or better-placed units may have more votes, for example. Alternatively, each unit may have one vote, regardless of size, location, or other factors.

The board establishes a budget and assumes responsibility for collecting fees, enforcing rules, deciding on repairs and improvements, and overseeing maintenance and administration of the facility. Depending on the size of the development, the board usually hires a management company to run the condo on a day-to-day basis, while the board oversees its management activities.

The board is, in effect, a mini-government. Its members determine condo policies on such issues as pets, renovations, and leasing units. If you don't make your payments on time, the board can put a lien against your property. What does this mean to you? A couple of things: before you buy a condo, be sure you understand the authority of the board and feel comfortable with this structure. If it bothers you that

### Rules Keep the Peace

Some rules are good! You may want your freedom, but you'll quickly find that a few rules are necessary when a family with 17 children, two aunts, one uncle, two grandpas, four dogs, and one cat moves into the two-bedroom unit next door, and they all think that fireworks every night are a great way to keep the kids entertained. Rules help to keep the peace in a condo community.

you have to get permission to renovate your bathroom, you may be frustrated with condominium living.

If you decide to purchase a condominium, it's a good idea to get to know the board members. The board members reflect the values and opinions of the other residents. Keep in mind that you'll be living closely with these residents. Are you comfortable with the philosophy? Do you fit in?

Be sure that you understand all the financial obligations that come with owning a condominium. The section "Making an Offer," later in this chapter, discusses this topic in more detail. For instance, you might want to find out about plans for improvements or major repairs. In some cases, the board can make the residents pay a special assessment for repairs and improvements.

## Selecting a Community

If you're considering a condo, the first aspect you should check out is the community. Here are some points to consider:

*Is the condo association financially sound?* You don't want to purchase a condo in a community where the treasurer has just absconded with all the condo fees. The association should keep a reserve of funds for repairs and improvements. If that reserve is empty, you as a condo owner can be charged a special assessment for repairs. Ask how many special assessments have been made in the past few years. Ask about any planned improvements or repairs and how they'll be financed.

*Is the condo well managed?* One of the benefits of living in a condo is leaving the maintenance up to the condo association and the company it hires to do the job. If the association doesn't do its job, and your grass grows up to your waist, what's the benefit?

*How many condos are sold?* Vacant? Rented? If many of the condos are sold, it may indicate a solid community. If many are vacant, you should wonder why. Also, if many are vacant, that means there's less money in the maintenance kitty.

*Which facilities are part of the community?* Is there a gym, swimming pool, meeting rooms? Are you part owner of the facilities, or do you have to pay a fee to use them? Make sure the facilities are adequate for the community. That pool may look nice now, but when all 200 kids from the community pile in, the pool won't look so attractive.

*What by-laws and restrictions must you obey?* Can you have a dog? Can you paint your garage a different color? You should look closely at the master deed, which should list the conditions, covenants, and restrictions of the development. Read the by-laws to see who's responsible for what. What authority does the board have?

*What are the monthly charges for the condo association fees?*

# Checking Out the Condominium

In addition to looking at the community, you should carefully check out the unit itself. Is it well maintained? What's the square footage? What amenities are included? Do you like the floor plan?

# Making an Offer

Before you make an offer, you should review the master deed, by-laws, and house rules carefully with your agent and/or lawyer. If you don't review these documents before making the offer, you should make the review and acceptance of these documents a contingency in the contract.

### Your Rights

You can't be turned down for housing based on race, gender, or national origin. If you think you have encountered discrimination, you can contact your provincial human rights authority.

The sales contract is similar to a single-family home contract. The contract includes the offer price, the terms, and any contingencies. (Information on drawing up and negotiating a contract can be found in Chapters 8 and 9.)

Getting financing on a condominium is similar to getting financing on a house. One difference is that the lender will include your monthly condo association fee as part of your PITI (principal, interest, taxes, and insurance). Also, you may be required to make a larger down payment. Finally, some lenders may make loans only for approved condos.

## More on Financing

We'll cover financing your home in more detail in the next chapter. For now, though, you should know about a few wrinkles that affect the financing of a new condominium unit. If you're buying a new unit, the builder probably has obtained a blanket mortgage over the entire development. The builder uses this mortgage loan to pay the tradesmen and contractors who work on the project. As the builder sells each unit of the project, his lender reduces the scope of the blanket mortgage accordingly (and usually tries to sign up the purchaser of each unit for a conventional mortgage on the individual units).

However, there's a period between the time you close the deal and the time you actually take possession of your condo when the builder still holds title to the property. During this period, you pay the builder a monthly occupancy fee. When the deal finally closes and title to the individual condominium unit passes to you, you pay the builder the outstanding amount on the price of your condo, either from your own resources or with a mortgage loan.

## Buying a Co-op

In some ways, a co-operative (or co-op) is similar to a condominium. The key difference is in the structure of ownership. Rather than owning real estate, you buy shares in a corporation that owns the building. When you purchase a certain number of shares, you then have the right to live in a particular unit. This is called a proprietary lease. Unlike buying a condominium, which you can do if you have the money, buying a co-op requires prior approval by the co-op's board. As a private organization, board members can reject your application to buy shares for all sorts of reasons, and they don't have to tell them to you. Sound snobby? It can be.

In Canada, most co-ops are found in Toronto, but you may also find this type of living arrangement in other large cities, such as Montreal or Vancouver.

## Financing Your Co-op

To get approval on most co-op loans, a lender requires that the participating co-op meet certain standards: structural soundness, restricted commercial use, fiscally responsible budget, and good management. You can expect to pay a higher interest rate on a co-op loan, but the closing costs may be less. You may also be required to make a higher down payment, usually as much as 50% of the total price. That's because the lender would have more trouble reselling a co-op unit than a condo or a house if you were to default on the loan.

Your monthly payment includes your monthly maintenance fee. A lender will probably include this fee in your total monthly payment when qualifying you for a loan.

In addition to satisfying the lender's criteria, you'll also have to pass inspection from the board members. You may need to submit personal references and financial statements. The board may also interview you.

## Selecting a Co-Op

Selecting a co-op is similar to selecting a condominium. You should investigate the building and management carefully. You should review the proprietary lease, by-laws, and financial statements of the corporation. Here are some items to consider:

*Is the co-op financially sound?* Do they meet all the expenses for running a co-op? Do they have reserves to cover renovations and repairs?

*How old is the building?* Does it need repairs? New roof? New elevators? You may want to have a co-op professionally inspected.

*What covenants, conditions, and regulations do you have to observe?* You should know the rules you must follow. You should also investigate whether you can sublet the unit.

## The Least You Need to Know

Many first-time buyers or retiring couples decide to purchase a condominium rather than a single-family home. In big cities such as Toronto, you may also find people who own a co-op, which is a different form of home ownership.

➤ The term condominium refers not to the style of home, but to the form of ownership. When you own a condo, you don't own the walls, floors, or ceilings of your unit. Instead, you own the airspace within those walls. You may also own a part of the common facilities.

➤ If you live in a condominium, you don't have to worry about maintenance. Instead, you pay a monthly fee, and someone else maintains the property. This monthly fee varies depending on the community.

➤ When you purchase a co-op, you don't own property. Instead, you own shares in the corporation that owns the co-op. In return for the shares, the corporation grants you a proprietary lease, which gives you the right to live in a certain unit.

➤ Be sure to check out the condominium or co-op by-laws, rules, restrictions, and other management and financial information. You should select a community that's financially sound and well managed.

# Chapter 12

# Getting Financing

## In this chapter
➤ Understanding how lending works
➤ Understanding mortgages
➤ Selecting a lender
➤ Applying for a mortgage

Once the seller has accepted your offer, you have a piece of paper saying you're buying that property. Now you have to put your money on the line. For most of us, that means getting the financing in order.

This chapter assumes that you're not independently wealthy and probably need a loan to pay for your new home. It discusses the types of financing available and what you have to do to get a mortgage.

## How Lending Works

Banking is a business, just like any other, involving buying and selling. What bankers and other lenders sell is money.

Here's one example of how it works: your Aunt Betty deposits $500 in her savings account, and the bank agrees to pay her 2% interest on her money. The bankers then take Aunt Betty's $500 and lend it to you. In exchange for letting you use the money, the bank charges you 7% interest.

The 7% interest rate covers the 2% the bank has to pay Aunt Betty, the cost of moving the money around, and a profit for the bank. The difference between the savings interest and lending interest is called the *spread*.

When money is tight, more people want money, and rates go up. When money isn't tight, there's more money than there are borrowers, and rates go down.

## Principal: The Big Kahuna

Unless you have enough money of your own to pay for a property, you'll have to borrow some money while using your own money as a down payment. The amount you borrow is called the principal of the mortgage. As you repay the loan over time, the amount of the principal declines.

## Interest Rates, or What's the Charge?

If all lenders offered money to all buyers at the same rates and on the same terms, selecting a lender would be easy. But lending is a business, and lenders compete for your business by adjusting the terms of a loan. How much you pay for the loan, how often you pay and over how long a period can vary from one lender to the next.

Lenders differ in how much they charge you to use their money. This charge, called the *interest rate*, depends on the lender, the economy, the type of loan, and other factors. The interest rate has a huge effect on how much you pay for an item.

If you borrow $100,000 at 7% for 25 years, your monthly payment will be $701. If you borrow the same amount of money for the same amount of time but at 10%, your payment increases to $895 a month. The difference is $194 a month.

## Amortization: Everything You Need to Know in Three Sentences

The lender calculates your monthly payments based on the total length of time it will take to pay the mortgage in full. The customary amortization period is 25 years, but you can arrange for shorter amortization periods as well. The shorter the amortization period, the larger your payments, but the more you save on interest.

Over a 25-year amortization period, for example, a borrower would make 300 payments. Over a ten-year amortization, the borrower would make only 120 payments, but each payment would be much larger.

## Term: If the Amortization Period Is the School Year, the Term Is One Semester

Mortgage lenders provide money for a certain period, ranging from six months to ten years. This period is called the term of the mortgage. If you think interest rates will soon fall, you might want a short-term mortgage. If you think they're going to remain steady or go up, you might want a longer-term mortgage.

At the end of the term, the principal and interest on the mortgage come due. Unless your Great Uncle Hughie dies and leaves you an oil well so you can pay off the mortgage, you'll likely renew it with the same lender or look around for another lender who can give you a better deal.

> **Short but Sweet**
>
> On a $100,000 mortgage, at 7% interest, amortized over 25 years, you'd make a monthly payment of $701. Amortized over 15 years, you'd pay $894 a month. But it would take you ten years less to pay off your mortgage, and you'd save more than $20,000 over the entire amortization period.

## Types of Financing

My mom and dad live in the same house as I grew up in. They've been paying for the house for almost 25 years. They pay the same monthly payment now as they did in 1975, when they bought the house. (Their house payment is less than my car payment!) Back when they purchased their home, most people selected this type of financing, which is called fixed-rate financing. Most people expected to stay in their homes for 25 years and wanted the stability of fixed payments.

Times have changed! First, people don't stay in the same spot so long and, second, lenders have become more creative with the financ-

## Death Grip

The word **mortgage** is derived from the Latin word meaning "dead" (*mortuum*) and the Old Teutonic word meaning "pledge" (*wadjo*, which also provides the root for "wage"). Writing in the 17th century, the English jurist and legal scholar Lord Coke suggested that the word came into being because, if the individual providing the pledge defaults on the mortgage, the property used to secure the mortgage "is taken from him forever" and so "becomes dead to him." Now you know.

ing they offer. Now you can shop around for different types of loans.

Mortgage loans vary depending on who offers the loan and how it's backed. The two most common types of loans are conventional and government-assisted. You can get your loans from Bill Banker or from Bill Banker with Ottawa backing you. Loans also vary depending on how the payments are structured. The two most common structures are fixed-rate mortgages and variable-rate mortgages.

A mortgage actually consists of two legal documents: The note specifies the amount of the loan, the repayment terms and other conditions of the agreement; the mortgage itself gives the lender claim to the property if the borrower defaults.

# Conventional Loans

I'm not sure where the term "conventional" originated. Perhaps this term got tagged on this type of loan because most conventional loans are made by bankers, and bankers are known to be conservative, traditional, yes, even conventional. Think blue suits, white shirts, boring ties.

Conventional loans are secured from a lender, usually a bank or trust company. Conventional loans require a down payment of at least 25% of the price of the home. The value is determined by an appraisal or by the purchase price, whichever is less.

# High-Ratio/Insured Mortgage

If you can't scrape together 25% of the cost of the home, you might still qualify for a high-ratio mortgage, insured by the Canada Mortgage and Housing Corporation (CMHC), a crown corporation, or the Mortgage Insurance Company of Canada, a private company. You can obtain up to 95% of the purchase price, depending on the price of the house, whether you've bought another home within the last five years, and other conditions.

The insurance protects lenders. It enables them to lend money to people who might not qualify for a mortgage under ordinary circumstances. To obtain a conventional uninsured mortgage, for example, a borrower needs enough money for a down payment of 25% or more of the value of a property. Some people don't have that much cash available. By applying for an insured mortgage, they can still buy a home. The borrower's happy; the lender's happy; and everyone wins.

Depending on the amount of personal money you use for a down payment, you'll have to pay an application fee of $75 to $235 and a premium of 0.50% to 2.50% of your loan to obtain a CMHC-insured mortgage.

# Vendor Take-Back Mortgage

Sometimes vendors will offer to help potential purchasers who want to buy a property by lending them a portion of the purchase price. Called a vendor-take-back (VTB) mortgage or purchase mortgage, such a loan often comes with favorable or flexible terms, depending on the inclinations of the individual vendor. The loan may be open, for example, which means you can repay the loan at any time, without penalty. The vendor may charge an interest rate lower than the prevailing market rate. Or the vendor may negotiate with you about the term of the loan.

By obtaining a VTB mortgage, you can avoid a lot of red tape and administrative charges. You don't have to sit in a bank, waiting for a loans officer to look you over and examine your credentials before approving your mortgage. You can sit down with another person at the kitchen table and work out the specific details of your loan, without waiting for approval from a higher authority.

# Open and Closed Mortgages

With a fully open mortgage, you can pay off all or part of your mortgage at any time during the term of the loan, without penalty. In return for this privilege, you'll likely incur a slightly higher interest rate. If you have a fully open mortgage and interest rates fall below the rate that you're currently paying, you can refinance at a lower rate, without penalty.

During the 1980s and early 1990s, interest rates fluctuated drastically. As a result, most lenders stopped offering open mortgages, because they wanted to maintain some stability and predictability within their own loan portfolios. With interest rates stabilizing, however, a few lenders have started offering two-year or three-year open mortgages. Many more offer open mortgages for very short terms of six months or less.

Some lenders offer partially open mortgages that allow you to repay a portion of the mortgage without penalty. Others will negotiate a prepayment penalty in advance, so you'll know, for example, that you have to pay an additional three months' interest if you prepay your mortgage.

A closed mortgage restricts the borrower from refinancing, repaying or making other changes to a mortgage agreement over the full term of the loan. Even if interest rates fall below the rate of the loan, the borrower must continue to repay the mortgage at the higher rate until the mortgage comes up for renewal. If you sell your property and can't transfer the mortgage, you'll have to negotiate with the lender and hope you can repay the mortgage at all.

To pay off a closed mortgage, you'll almost certainly have to pay a penalty. The penalty usually amounts to three months of payments, but the lender can charge more or refuse to let you pay off the mortgage at all.

Some mortgage agreements allow you to prepay a certain percentage of your mortgage, but not the entire mortgage. Under the terms of some mortgages, you can pay off the balance only after you've repaid a specified proportion of the principal. Others allow you to pay off a percentage of the total loan once a year, but not the remaining balance.

You should make sure that your agreement covers both portions. If it allows you to repay 10% or 15% a year prematurely and without penalty, for example, what penalty will you incur if you prepay the

**Prepayment Blues**

If your mortgage agreement doesn't specify the penalty you incur if you prepay the entire amount before it comes due, you could have a problem if you sell your home in the meantime. You might have to pay a penalty of three months' interest or more. In some cases, the lender may not let you prepay the mortgage at all. So you could sell your house and still have a mortgage to pay.

remainder? Don't neglect this portion of the agreement until you need it. By then, it will be too late to negotiate.

## Fixed vs. Floating Rate

With a fixed rate, the interest rate that you pay on your mortgage remains stable over the entire term of the mortgage. A floating rate fluctuates according to the prevailing interest rate set by the Bank of Canada.

Individuals who think mortgage rates might drop usually choose a floating rate; others who think interest rates might rise select a fixed rate, which protects them from the impact of rising interest rates. But certainty comes with a price: a fixed-rate mortgage usually carries a higher interest rate than a floating-rate mortgage.

## Variable-Rate Mortgage

With a variable rate mortgage, you pay interest at the prevailing rate each month, although you make a fixed monthly payment over the term of the

**Refinancing Can Pay** WHOA!

If you have a fixed-rate loan, you may not be stuck with that loan for the rest of your life. You can refinance the loan to get a better interest rate. Generally, it's a good idea to refinance if interest rates drop by 2% or more.

You'll likely have to pay a penalty if you refinance before the term of your mortgage ends. But calculate the costs to see how long you must have the new loan to break even on the cost of refinancing.

agreement. This means that the proportion of principal and interest changes from one payment to the next. Your monthly interest is calculated according to the prime rate. If interest rates go up, your payments remain the same, but the additional interest is added to your total debt. If interest rates go down, your payments remain the same, but the amount that goes toward the principal increases.

You can pay off all or some of a variable-rate mortgage at any time, usually without penalty, or convert it to a fixed-rate mortgage at any time.

**Only in Canada**

A uniquely Canadian concept, a **convertible mortgage** usually carries the lowest interest rate of any available mortgage. You pay interest at a fixed rate over a short term of no more than six months. As with a variable-rate mortgage, you can convert the mortgage at no cost to a longer, closed fixed-term mortgage at any time.

With a convertible mortgage, your repayments are applied to principal and interest in equal proportions over the entire term, even if interest rates fluctuate.

## Portability

Some mortgage lenders allow you to take your mortgage with you if you buy a new home before the mortgage's term expires. This can save you money in several ways: first, you avoid a penalty for paying off your current mortgage prematurely. Second, you avoid paying any fees involved in discharging the mortgage. Third, you avoid many of the costs involved in obtaining a new mortgage.

If your new home requires a larger mortgage, you can add the required amount to the existing mortgage and blend the interest rates to determine your total monthly payment.

## Increased Payments

Some lenders allow you to increase the size of your monthly payments by a certain percentage at any time during the term of the mortgage. This is similar to making an annual lump-sum payment, except you spread the payments over 12 months. The additional amount goes toward the principal of your mortgage, which considerably reduces the amount of interest you pay over the life of the mortgage. You should make sure this privilege is described in writing in your mortgage agreement.

# Do You Qualify?

Institutional lenders such as banks, insurance companies, and trust companies will usually lend up to 75% of the appraised value of a home in the form of a conventional first mortgage. In most cases, your Gross Debt Service (GDS) Ratio — your monthly payments on a conventional first mortgage, plus property taxes and heating costs — can't exceed about one-third of your total monthly income. Your Total Debt Service (TDS) Ratio — your GDS plus payments on all other debts — can't exceed about 40% of your total monthly income.

If you're applying for a government-insured loan, you'll need a down payment of 10% of the home's appraised value. (Qualified first-time buyers need only 5%.) Under Canada Mortgage and Housing Corporation guidelines, you can't devote more than 32% of your gross household income toward the payment of the mortgage principal plus interest, property taxes, heat, and 50% of condo fees, if applicable. Nor can you commit more than 40% of your total household income to your total debt repayment, including mortgage principal, interest, property taxes, heat, plus 50% of condo fees if applicable, plus payment on all other debts such as credit cards, car loans, and leases.

# Optimal Size of Mortgage

Most lenders will provide a mortgage whose monthly payments, including principal, interest, taxes, and heat, require no more than one-third of your total income. Within this limit, the size of the mortgage you negotiate will depend on your current and future income, your credit rating, your tolerance for debt, and your outlook on the property market.

If you think you'll earn an increasing amount of money every year, then the size of your mortgage will fall in proportion to your total income. Presumably, this will make it less onerous to repay your mortgage as time passes. A large mortgage today may not seem so large in three or four years, as your income increases.

Some people simply don't like owing money to other people. They like to stay free of obligations, financial or otherwise. The larger their debt, the greater their discomfort. If you're one of them, a small mortgage makes sense. Likewise, if you feel unsure about your job and your income, however, you may choose a smaller mortgage to reduce your anxiety if the worst happens.

## Why It Can Pay to Borrow

When interest rates are low, you might consider borrowing as much money as you can to buy a house. That way, you'll get the highest return on your investment. In fact, you should never pay cash for a house, but use borrowed money instead, even if you have the cash available. Here's why:

If you pay $200,000 in cash to buy a house, and property values rise by 5% a year, your property will appreciate by 50% in ten years. It will be worth $300,000, and your equity will have increased by $100,000.

That may sound attractive, but you could have increased your equity even further by borrowing money to buy a bigger house. If you'd taken your $200,000, borrowed another $300,000, and bought a house worth $500,000, whose value appreciates at 5% a year, in ten years it would be worth $750,000. Your equity would increase by $250,000. By borrowing money, you'd have $150,000 more than you'd have if you'd paid cash.

If you expect property values to fall, however, you may think twice about borrowing a lot of money to buy a property. As we've mentioned, the farther the value of your property falls, the greater the proportion of your debt to your equity.

## Don't Forget the Hidden Costs

As part of your application for a mortgage, you commit to pay the lender's costs of preparing and registering the mortgage. These costs include application fees, appraisal costs, legal fees, and disbursements. Your lender will provide details of these costs when you apply for the mortgage.

Most of these costs can be incorporated into the loan, so that you don't have to make any unanticipated payments when you acquire the property. Of course, that just makes them less apparent; it doesn't make them less painful to pay.

➤ **Appraisal fee** Appraisal fees range from $150 to $500. Lenders don't usually provide a copy of the appraisal to the borrower, but you should ask anyway.

In some cases, a seller may commission a professional appraiser to evaluate the property before putting it on the market. If the lender will accept the appraisal, you may avoid the cost of obtaining another one.

➤ **Survey fee** A survey should cost $150 to $400. Lenders want a survey to confirm that the property you've used as collateral for your mortgage complies with all relevant by-laws, that new additions don't extend beyond the boundaries of the property or that a neighbor won't dispute those boundaries. In some cases, a lender will accept a survey provided by the seller of the property, if it's up to date. In other cases, you'll have to arrange for the survey, either yourself or through your lawyer.

➤ **Mortgage insurance** If you obtain a high-ratio mortgage, you'll have to pay about 0.5% to 2.5% of the total amount for mortgage insurance provided by the Canada Mortgage and Housing Corporation or the Mortgage Insurance Corporation of Canada. This guarantees the lender that the loan will be repaid even if you default. The premium is usually added proportionately to your monthly mortgage payment.

➤ **Mortgage life insurance** Lenders often provide optional mortgage life insurance. If you die, your mortgage will be paid off. As an alternative, you might choose to obtain term life insurance that pays a lump sum in the event of your death equivalent to the size of your mortgage. Mortgage life insurance covers the remaining principal and interest outstanding on your mortgage and declines as you pay down your mortgage. For about the same amount, you can obtain a term life policy that pays an amount equivalent to the original mortgage, even if you've paid off most of your mortgage before you die.

➤ **Fire insurance** Lenders require coverage of a mortgaged property against fire and damage. The policy must cover the replacement cost of the property and specify that the lender of the first mortgage has first rights to the proceeds of the policy. The mortgage lender will require proof of insurance before you receive any funds under the mortgage.

**Dig In**

Some lenders suggest strongly that a borrower use the lender's lawyer to execute the transaction. But it usually works to your advantage to use your own lawyer, and you should dig in your heels if the lender tries to talk you out of the idea.

➤ **Provincial fees**  Most provinces require a fee for registering a mortgage and for transferring title of the property. These fees will usually appear on your lawyer's bill, and can amount to $100 or more.

➤ **Land transfer tax**  While it has nothing to do with your mortgage, provinces apply a tax to property transactions called a land transfer tax. It's usually calculated as a percentage of the total cost of the property. In Ontario, for example, you'll pay 1% of the first $100,000, up to 4% of any amount over $400,000.

➤ **Legal fees**  Lawyers charge a fee equivalent to about $1^1/4\%$ of the price of an average house. They usually deduct their fees for preparing and filing mortgage documents directly from the mortgage loan.

➤ **Goods and Services Tax:**

You'll have to pay GST on your lawyer's services and on any other services involved in obtaining a mortgage. You also have to pay GST on a new house or condominium, but not on a resale property. If you live in the property, and you pay no more than $350,000 for it, you're eligible for a rebate. This will ultimately reduce the GST you pay to 4% of the total value. Ask your lawyer about the procedures involved in obtaining this rebate.

# How to Decide on the Type of Financing

Deciding on the type of loan you take depends on several factors, including your current financial situation and your future plans.

# How Much Can You Afford for a Down Payment?

Money, as usual, is the first consideration. If you have piles and piles of money sitting in your closet, you can pick and choose among the different lending options. If you're like most people, though, you probably have just a dinky little pile, and it affects the type of the loan you can get.

For example, conventional loans require a 25% down payment. If you can't come up with that amount, you have to consider a different type.

## How Much Can You Afford for a Monthly Payment?

You can adjust your monthly payments by selecting a loan with a lower interest rate or longer amortization or by putting more money down. By selecting a loan type with the lowest initial interest rate, you may qualify for the house.

For example, suppose that you can pay no more than $700 a month. This amount includes principal, interest, taxes, and insurance. A fixed-rate loan at 8% may require monthly payments of $733. You won't qualify for this type of loan.

On the other hand, if there's a variable-rate mortgage available at 6%, the monthly payment for principal and interest is $600. You could qualify.

# Condominium Mortgages

The purchaser of a condominium unit receives legal title to the unit as well as an undivided interest in the common areas of the development. An undivided interest gives a purchaser the legal right to sell his or her share of the common area without the consent of the other purchasers.

The first mortgage registered against the entire condominium project is a blanket mortgage. As we discussed earlier in this chapter, that means the mortgage is registered over the entire property. The blanket mortgage is placed on the project by the developer, who uses the funds from the mortgage to build the project. As the developer sells individual units, the mortgagor discharges the mortgage off the individual units. Meanwhile, the purchaser places a condominium mortgage on his or her title, if required.

The condominium mortgage resembles a conventional mortgage, with a few additional details. These include:

➤ a clause giving the lender the right to use the borrower's vote in the condominium corporation. The corporation operates and manages the development. Theoretically, the lender could participate in all meetings of the corporation and vote on all decisions. In practice, this seldom happens.

➤ a clause allowing the lender to pay the common area costs of the condominium if the borrower fails to pay them. The lender then adds these costs to the principal amount of the mortgage, which is repaid with interest.

➤ a clause giving the lender the right to demand that the borrower comply with all the terms of the condominium by-laws. By breaching any of the by-laws, the borrower also defaults on the mortgage.

## A Weighty Decision

Here the decision being weighed is the type of mortgage that's best for you. None at all would be best. But most of us don't have that option.

## Pluses

A fixed-rate mortgage gives you the benefit of knowing your exact payment for the term of the loan. What you pay on a ten-year loan in 1994 will be the same amount you pay in 2004. To some buyers, the financial security of having a set payment greatly outweighs any savings they might gain from getting another type of mortgage.

Fixed-rate mortgages are especially sensible when interest rates are low. Why take the chance of playing "spin the interest rate" when you can lock into a favorable rate now? If you plan to stay in your home for a long time, a fixed rate becomes even more desirable.

Finally, keep in mind that if your income is likely to rise, the burden of making payments will not be so great. While you're making twice the money, your house payments will still be the same as they were three years ago. That's a plus. And if your income is likely to decrease or remain steady (for instance, if you're retiring) a fixed-rate mortgage might also be the best bet. Your payments will be the same, so you can plan accordingly.

## Minuses

When interest rates are high, the picture changes. In this case, the rates for a fixed-rate mortgage may be so high that you can't qualify for a fixed-rate loan. Also, why lock into a higher rate for the life of the loan?

### Don't Lock Now

You don't save much money by locking in to a long--term mortgage, even when interest rates are rising. Economist Peter Norman compared home owners who obtained a mortgage in January 1987, when interest rates reached their lowest point in several years. On a mortgage of $122,700, the borrower who chose a five-year term at 10.75% ended up paying $52,216 in principal and interest. The borrower who chose five one-year terms, at interest rates of 9.5%, 10.25%, 12.13%, 12.65%, and 12.2%, paid $52,321, a difference of only $105 over five years. In the meantime, the borrower with the shorter terms could take full advantage of all available prepayment options.

During other periods, when interest rates were more volatile and did not rise or fall steadily, according to Norman's analysis, short-term borrowers saved as much as $28,000 by choosing a one-year term and renewing annually over five years, compared to borrowers who locked in to a five-year mortgage. When interest rates are low, Norman explains, more of your payment goes toward the principal.

Instead, consider a variable-rate mortgage, which is usually offered at a lower rate. If interest rates rise, you can convert the mortgage to a fixed rate, usually for a fee.

## Is the Shorter Amortization Better?

Some real estate professionals advise buyers to take a 15-year rather than a 25-year amortization. You end up saving a considerable sum if you stay in the home for a long period.

Other experts disagree. These experts say that you may not want to tie up your money for housing expenses. You can always make double payments on the 25-year loan, but if you find yourself in a financial bind, you're not locked in to these higher payments.

Or you can put the extra money in a savings account or mutual fund that earns more money than your mortgage rate. This leaves the money readily available in the event of an emergency.

Whether or not to go with a shorter amortization is up to you. If you can't afford or qualify for the higher payments of a 15-year loan, you should consider a 20- or 25-year loan. You'll still get to decide, though, how often you'd like to make those payments.

Biweekly payments can save you a lot of money, but they may also be more of a headache. You have to make twice as many payments, and some lenders charge a handling fee for this type of mortgage.

## Go Short

A short-term mortgage makes sense, especially if it's closed, because it gives you a chance to make a large repayment when the term expires without incurring a penalty. If you anticipate a large inheritance or a windfall from another source, you should choose a short-term mortgage, unless a lender will agree to an open mortgage.

## Prepaying Your Mortgage

When you're shopping around for a mortgage, inquire whether you can prepay the mortgage without penalty. Why prepay?

Remember that the lenders want their money first, so most of your money in the first few years of the loan goes toward interest.

On a $115,000 loan at 8%, for example, you pay around $10,000 in monthly payments in the first year, but less than $1,000 of that goes toward the principal. After one year, you still owe $114,000.

Here's where prepaying can be beneficial. When you prepay, the money goes directly to the principal. If you have an extra $1,000 after paying your monthly bills (yeah, right), you can pay that $1,000 toward the mortgage. That money goes directly toward the principal.

Again, financial experts disagree on whether prepaying the mortgage is beneficial or not. It does reduce the amount of money you pay for the home. You'll pay off the home more quickly if you prepay.

Critics of prepaying argue that you can put extra money to better use. For example, if you prepay that $1,000, you get no tax benefit. If you put that money into a registered retirement plan, you'll get a tax break. If you put the money into a savings account, you'll have access to it if you need it. If your mortgage rate is 7%, and you invest in a mutual fund paying 10%, you can make 3% on your money rather than paying off your mortgage.

Keep in mind that prepaying does not reduce your monthly payment obligations. You can't tell the lender that you paid an extra $1,000 last year, so this year you are going to skip the first few payments. You *must* still make the regular payments.

# Assumable Mortgages

Certain mortgages are *assumable*, which means the buyer can just assume the responsibilities of the seller's mortgage. The buyer doesn't have to pay for obtaining a new mortgage and, if the mortgage has a lower-than-market or reasonable interest rate, the buyer can save a lot of money on interest.

**Pay it Now, Pay It Fast**

It's a good idea to pay for your house and pay off your mortgage as quickly as you can. In this way, you pay as little interest as possible. That means you should take advantage of opportunities to make double-up payments and annual lump-sum payments.

For example, suppose that a seller has a 7% fixed-rate mortgage and has a buyer that is interested in assuming the payments on this loan. If the loan is freely assumable, the buyer can save the costs of applying for a loan and other associated costs. (The buyer usually must get the lender's approval for the loan.)

The buyer assumes payment on the existing mortgage and pays the difference between the mortgage balance and the selling price. For example, if the seller sold the home for $100,000 and still owed $80,000, the buyer would assume the $80,000 mortgage and pay the seller $20,000. You can see that even if you don't have the expense of closing on a loan, you may still have to come up with a considerable sum of cash. In this example, to raise the additional $20,000, the buyer could obtain a mortgage from the same lender, who would blend the rates and terms together with the assumable mortgage.

You may not want to assume a mortgage, but you'll want to ask whether the mortgage you're securing is assumable. An assumable mortgage may be more attractive to buyers when you sell your home.

# Selecting a Lender

A lot of buyers are grateful that someone is willing to lend them the money to buy a home, so they don't realize that they should shop around for a lender. Don't forget, you're a customer. You're giving the lender your business, and you should be sure to select the lender that offers you the best deal and best service. The mortgage process can make or break a transaction.

# Who's Got the Money?

It can get confusing when you apply for a loan. There are so many lenders to choose from. A mortgage broker may interview you, then submit your application to another lender. Or your local bank branch may provide you with a loan. Here are some common sources of loans:

➤ commercial banks

➤ trust companies

➤ credit unions

➤ insurance companies

➤ Canada Mortgage and Housing Corporation (CMHC)

➤ vendor take-back

➤ personal sources

➤ mortgage brokers

# Mortgage Brokers

A mortgage broker is an intermediary who matches the particular needs of a borrower with the specific criteria of a lender. There are more than 2,500 of them in Canada, primarily in B.C., Alberta, Ontario, and Quebec.

In addition to dealing with conventional lenders such as banks, trust companies, and insurance companies, mortgage brokers also have access to sources of funds that aren't always apparent to the individual borrower, such as pension funds, private lenders, foreign banks, and syndicates of investors who regard mortgages as a secure form of investment.

In the past, borrowers used the services of a mortgage broker if they had problems finding a lender on their own. More recently, however, individuals have started to rely on mortgage brokers to mediate on their behalf, just as home buyers rely on real estate agents to help them buy and sell property. A qualified mortgage broker can negotiate more effectively than the average loan applicant — especially a first-time home buyer — who doesn't spend every day keeping track of all the bells and whistles that mortgage lenders use to attract customers and who may not have much experience in evaluating mortgage programs.

Before the borrower signs the mortgage papers, a broker must disclose in writing all the fees, costs, and deductions associated with the loan. For conventional mortgages, brokers do not charge the borrower a fee. Instead, they receive their payment from the lender. For borrowers who may not qualify for a conventional mortgage, however, a broker charges a fee of 1% to 2% of the mortgage itself. The broker usually collects the fee only after finding an acceptable mortgage.

# Mortgages on the Internet

Canada's major banks all operate Web sites on the Internet that answer questions about mortgages, calculate mortgage payments according to several variables such as amortization, interest rate, and frequency of payment, and determine the maximum loan for which you can qualify. The Canada Mortgage and Housing Corporation also operates a Web site describing CMHC's products, including its mortgage loan insurance programs (www.cmhc-schl.gc.ca).

In February 1997, CIBC (http://www.cibc.com) and Bank of Montreal (http://www.bmo.ca/mortgage) posted online mortgage applications on their Web sites that enable potential borrowers to apply for mortgage approval over the Internet. Borrowers can complete a mortgage application in about 45 minutes, then send it to the bank by e-mail or fax and receive a response within two days. Or they can take it in person to the nearest bank branch and get an immediate response. Royal Bank now provides a similar service (http://www.royalbank.com).

Through another Web site operated by a national mortgage brokerage called The Mortgage Centre (http://www.mortgagecentre.com), you can submit your mortgage application to the Mortgage Market and receive bids for your evaluation from major banks, trust companies, and life insurance companies.

In March 1997, Royal LePage Ltd. set up a similar service that lets a customer shop for a mortgage through the company's electronic network. The customer has to go to a Royal LePage office. By telephone or video teleconferencing system, the customer provides relevant information to a Royal LePage mortgage specialist. Within four hours, the customer can choose from the nine lending institutions that bid on the mortgage.

The nine lenders are:

1. The Associates — Ford Motor Credit (USA)

2. Beneficial Canada

3. CIBC Mortgage Corporation

4. Cooperative Trust — a collection of credit unions across Canada

5. First Line Trust — CIBC

6. M.R.S. Trust — Mackenzie group of funds

7. Mutual Group — Mutual Life of Canada

8. National Bank of Canada

9. Sun Life Trust — Sun Life Insurance

Meanwhile, through Online Mortgage Explorer Inc. (http://www.themortgage.com), you can fill in an electronic form, answer about 20 questions, and find out if you qualify for a mortgage from the Mutual Group, a group of 18 companies that offer financial services in Canada and the U.S.

Mortgage-related Web sites seem to be appearing almost daily. You can locate them through Yahoo Canada (http://www.yahoo.ca) or another search engine.

# Applying for the Mortgage

Once you select a lender, you face the agonizing process of applying for the loan. First, you have to gather and complete so much information. You may think you need everything from your second grade report card to your library card to secure a loan.

Second, you're bombarded with foreign terms and concepts dealing with financing. You should be a step ahead here, though.

Third, you have to wait. Waiting for approval is the worst.

# But Officer...

Depending on the type of lender you approach, you can expect to deal with a loan officer. This person is responsible for taking down all your financial information and is usually your primary contact at the bank, trust company, or credit union. This person makes sure that all the needed information is ready for review.

# How the Lender Decides Whether to Lend You Money

How does a lender decide that Buyer A gets the loan, but Buyer B is rejected? The lender will look at a number of factors, including your current financial situation, your payment history, the current lending guidelines, and the property being purchased.

Here's the basic process the lender goes through: the lender takes your application, verifies your employment and income information and source of down payment, checks your credit report and appraisal, and finally, approves or rejects the loan.

## Taking the Application

In the application process, the lender will ask you for a lot of information about your financial situation, such as your current income, your current debt obligations, and more.

Here are some of the things you'll have to provide:

➤ Copies of all bank statements (savings and checking) for the past three months. If an account shows a large deposit in the past few months, be prepared to explain where this money came from.

➤ Copies of all stock accounts and other assets (life insurance).

➤ Your most recent pay stubs as well as the names and addresses of your past employers.

➤ Your tax returns for the past two years. If you're self-employed, you'll need to provide additional tax returns and all your schedules, including profit and loss statements for past years as well as year-to-date.

➤ A copy of the purchase agreement. You may also need a copy of the front and back of the cheque for the deposit.

➤ If you're selling your current home to buy a new one, you'll need a copy of the listing agreement. If you've sold your house, bring a copy of the purchase agreement.

➤ If you're making the down payment with money given to you as a gift, you may be required to bring a gift letter, which states the money is a gift and does not have to be repaid.

➤ It's a good idea to bring a list of your addresses for the past five to ten years. You'll be asked to complete this information on the application.

➤ Collect the addresses and account numbers for all credit cards and other debts. For example, if you have a car loan, you'll need the lender's name, account number, and address. You should also know the monthly payments and balance owed.

➤ If you're renting, bring in copies of the past 12 months' rent cheques.

➤ If you have credit problems, be prepared to explain them.

## Verifying Information

The lender then reviews and verifies your information. Have you been employed at the place you listed for the amount of time you said? Is your salary what you say it is? Do you have a serious criminal record? Do you have the money you say you do in your bank or other accounts?

Accuracy is the key. The lender wants first to be sure the information is accurate, and second, to be sure that the information is honest (so if you want the loan, it's best to tell the truth).

If you have more than enough assets, you may not want to list them all. If you do, the lender will have to validate each asset you list, which can be time-consuming. Instead, list only enough to qualify for the loan and down payment you want. If it turns out you need additional assets to qualify, you can always mention them later.

## Credit Report

In addition to verifying your income and employment, the lender will order a credit report. This report will tell the lender about your credit rating and credit history. How have you managed past debts? Have you recently filed for bankruptcy? The lender will look for any trouble signs,

### Check Your Own Credit

You can obtain your own credit history by contacting the companies that compile such documents. Usually you'll need photocopies of two pieces of identification, along with proof of your current address, taken from a utility bill or credit card invoice. Mail this information to: Equifax Canada Inc., Box 190, Jean-Talon Station, Montreal, Quebec, H1S 2Z2, or Trans Union Consumer Relations Department, P.O. Box 338-LCD1, Hamilton, Ontario, L8L 7W2. They will mail the appropriate information to you in about two weeks.

such as a history of late or missed payments, and will check to see whether you listed all your debts. Not including some debts on an application can raise a red flag to the lender.

Finally, the lender will check to be sure you don't have *too much* credit available. Lenders may think that too much credit can be too tempting.

It's a good idea to check and clean up any credit problems before you apply for a loan. This topic is covered in Chapter 3. Also, most lenders run two credit checks (an initial check at the time of application and one later, right before closing.) For this reason, it's not a good idea to take on any new debt during the loan process. That debt is likely to show up on your second credit report.

## Getting an Appraisal

In addition to checking out *you*, the lender will also check out the property you intend to purchase. You may be silly enough to pay $125,000 for a house that's worth only $75,000, but the lender isn't going to lend you the money to do it. All loans require an independent appraisal, which you as buyer usually pay for. The appraiser determines the market value of the home.

To determine the value, the appraiser will look at the neighborhood. How many homes are currently on the market? How desirable is the area? The appraiser will also look closely at the condition of the home, the size and number of rooms, the type of construction, and the

### The Four Cs of Lending

If you've ever shopped for a diamond, you may know that the four Cs determine a diamond's worth. Lenders also use four Cs to qualify an individual for a loan.

*Capacity*. Will you be able to repay the debt? Lenders base the answer to this question on your current income and employment record. Lenders also look at your other financial obligations.

*Credit history*. Being able to repay the debt doesn't mean you *will repay* the debt. Lenders look at your past record of making payments. Did you make them on time?

*Capital*. How much money do you have right now? The lender will look at your assets. For instance, do you have money for the down payment? Do you have enough money after paying the down payment and closing costs or will you have to scrape by for a few months?

*Collateral*. What can the lender get from you if you default on the loan? The house, of course, but lenders want to ensure the house is worth the amount you're paying, hence the appraisal.

condition of the property. After reviewing the home and property, the appraiser will provide a value as well as supporting information on how that value was reached.

Request a copy of the appraisal in writing from the lender at the time of the application. This appraisal can give you solid information that backs up the value of the home. Note that you can't get the appraisal until the closing.

Usually, the lender hires the services of the appraiser, and you pay for the appraisal through the lender.

## Approving or Denying the Loan

Once he has all the details about your income information, credit history, appraisal, and so on, the lender will decide whether to give you the loan.

If the loan is approved, you should receive a commitment letter stating the loan amount, amortization, term, interest rate, and the monthly payment. If you agree to these terms, you sign the letter. If you don't, you shake hands, say goodbye, and go somewhere else.

Read the commitment letter carefully. Lenders sometimes make mistakes. You'll want to be sure the terms are exactly as you intended. If the letter is not accurate, do not sign it.

If the loan is not approved, your loan officer will let you know. See the section "What to Do if Your Loan Is Not Approved."

# Preapproval

What if rates rise or fall during the period when you're looking for a home? To eliminate this uncertainty, most lenders will preapprove a mortgage, based on the criteria that we've just described, but without the appraisal.

The lender's preapproval should protect you from any increase in interest rates during a specified period, usually 90 days. It should also allow you to take advantage of a decline in interest rates. This may seem obvious, but some lenders, especially private ones, don't always extend this consideration to preapproved borrowers.

Some institutional lenders allow an unlimited number of adjustments, while others restrict the number of interest-rate adjustments they'll allow after they provide their preapproval. In some cases, a lender will reduce the interest rate on a preapproved mortgage but will charge the borrower an administrative fee. Rather than paying such a fee, you should look for another lender, unless there are other, more compelling reasons not to change.

Even with a preapproved mortgage, you should not be surprised if the price that you've offered on a property differs from the lender's appraised value. As we've explained, lenders tend to be conservative in their evaluations of property. If the appraised value is lower than the price that you've offered for the property, you'll need a larger down payment.

# Ensuring a Smooth Process

You may feel as if the entire loan process is out of your hands. That out-of-control feeling can be uncomfortable when so much is at stake.

There are some things that you can do to ensure a smooth loan process:

*Clean up your credit report.* Be sure to clear up any credit problems before you apply for a loan. If problems turn up later, a lender won't want to hear your explanation after the fact.

*Provide all requested information quickly.* If the loan officer asks you for a pay stub, get the stub to her as quickly as possible.

*Get copies of everything to protect yourself.* For instance, if you locked in a rate, get it in writing.

*Call your loan officer periodically to check on the progress.* If there are problems, you should know immediately, not at the end of 60 days. Perhaps the lender requires additional documentation. You should make sure there are no holdups that you're responsible for.

*Don't make any big purchases right before or during the loan process.* If you go out and buy a new car right before you apply for a loan, that debt will show up on your record. If you buy the car after you apply, the debt may also show up, because most lenders run *two* credit checks: one when you apply and one right before the closing. So if you're contemplating a big purchase, it's best to wait till after your loan is approved.

# What to Do if You Can't Get a Loan

If you're denied a loan, the lender will usually explain the decision, often in writing. You should talk to the loan officer and find out what went wrong. If you can clear up the problem, the lender may reconsider. If not, you may have to secure other financing.

Ask the loan officer for suggestions on how to improve your chances of getting approved. A loan officer has experience dealing with many successful and unsuccessful loans. He may be able to give you some advice on improving your chances.

Sometimes the institution itself simply doesn't want to lend money on the conditions or terms that you require. If that's the case, the lending officer will tell you, and you should go to another lender.

The following section discusses some of the problems that can cause a loan to be denied.

# Income Problems

If you don't have enough income to qualify for that loan, you can try the following to correct this situation:

*Secure other financing.* If you can't obtain financing through a traditional lender, you may try a different type of financing. Maybe the seller can help you with financing. Also, you should ask your agent for suggestions.

*Point out extenuating circumstances to the lender.* For example, if you're about to get a raise, you may ask your employer to give the lender a letter saying so. This may improve your financial picture enough to qualify.

*Shop for a less expensive home.* If you can't qualify for a mortgage on the home of your dreams, perhaps you can qualify for a less expensive home and then trade up when you're more financially secure.

*Start a savings program.* If you don't have enough for the down payment, start saving now. You may not be able to afford a house today, but that will change if you save enough. Create a budget and start saving money for your home. You could even consider taking a second job temporarily. You could determine the amount you have to save for a down payment, then deposit each pay check from your second job directly into your savings account. When you reach your savings goal, quit your second job and start looking for that dream home!

*Examine your current debts.* If that dream home is important enough to you, try lowering your existing debts by making some sacrifices. You could trade in your car for a less expensive model; you could sell one car if your family has more than one, then car pool or take public transportation; you could consolidate some outstanding loans so your monthly payments are lower. Be creative and brutal. Trim the fat. If you're spending a lot each month on concerts, movies, or restaurants, cut back. You'll be surprised how quickly all of this adds up.

# Credit Problems

If your credit report comes back with problems, you should ask to see a copy. If there are errors, have them corrected. If there are problems, correct them or add your explanation. Doing so may or may not change the lender's mind.

If you have too much debt to qualify for a loan, consider paying off some of the debts if you can. If you can't, but have a good credit history, ask the lender to reconsider.

If you have serious debt-management problems, consider getting some financial counseling.

## Appraisal Problems

Most lenders will give you a loan for only a certain percentage of the appraised value. If the appraisal is higher than what you're paying, you won't have to worry. If the appraisal is less, you will qualify for a smaller mortgage. In this case, you can come up with a larger down payment to cover the difference. Or, if you made the sale contingent on an acceptable appraisal, you may be able to renegotiate the price.

# The Least You Need to Know

Mortgage loans vary on interest rates, amortization, terms, and other factors.

➤ Fixed-rate loans are a good idea when interest rates are low, when you plan to stay in your house for a while, or if you do not like taking risks.

➤ With a variable-rate mortgage, the portion of your payment that goes toward the principal and the interest varies according to the prevailing interest rate.

➤ Be sure to ask whether you can prepay on the loan without penalty.

➤ Prepaying reduces the principal (the amount you owe) more quickly than just making regular payments.

➤ A lender will verify your financial information, check your credit history, order an appraisal on the property, then approve or deny the loan.

➤ You'll most likely be charged a fee for an appraisal. The appraiser will look at the home and property and determine its current market value.

➤ In qualifying you for a loan, the lender will decide whether you can and will pay. The lender will also look at the cash you have now and the collateral you'll have in case you default on the loan.

➤ A loan may not be approved for one of several reasons, including insufficient income, a bad credit report, and a low appraisal.

**We must be the worst family in town.
Maybe we should move to a larger
community.**

—Bart Simpson
(Matt Groening)

# Part III
# Close on the House

*The final step in buying a house is the closing. This part covers the key steps you need to follow in getting to that final goal — owning your home. In particular, you need to arrange for insurance, have an inspection done, sign lots and lots of documents (be sure to read the fine print), hand over all your money, then finally, finally get the keys to your new house so you can move in and begin paying for it.*

JIMMY DIDN'T READ THE FINE PRINT.

"IT'S COOL IN THE SUMMER!"... YOU IDIOT.

WINICK

# Insurance

When I started to write this chapter, I thought about the things that can happen to a home, and then, like most people, I figured that home damage wasn't all that common.

Then I started researching what's covered and what isn't covered in a policy, and I thought about articles in the local paper in the past year or so. Someone's house burnt down. Someone drove his car into a person's living room. A plane landed on a house. Hail broke all the windows in a house. Accidents do happen, even though we don't like to think that they'll happen to us.

Insurance protects you from many different kinds of risks. When you purchase a home, you'll need to purchase a different type of insurance for each of these risks, as covered in this chapter.

# Understanding Types of Insurance

Thinking of insuring a home, you probably think immediately of home owner's insurance. But there are actually several types of insurance — two that you'll definitely need and one that the lender may require:

*Home owner's insurance* covers your home, your possessions, and people on your property. Your lender will require it.

*Mortgage insurance* protects the lender in case you default on the loan. If you need a high-ratio mortgage, you'll have to pay for mortgage insurance.

*Mortgage life insurance* covers the outstanding principal and interest on your mortgage and declines as you pay down your mortgage. It's optional.

### The 11 Common Perils

The most basic home owner's policy covers what are known as the 11 common perils. More expensive policies cover these basics, plus others.

➤ Fire or lightning

➤ Loss of property because of fire or other perils

➤ Windstorm or hail

➤ Explosion

➤ Riots and other civil commotions

➤ Aircraft

➤ Vehicles

➤ Smoke

➤ Vandalism and malicious mischief

➤ Theft

➤ Breakage of glass that constitutes a part of the building.

# Getting Home Insurance

Most people don't like to think about bad things happening, and rightly so. Still, they happen, and you should be prepared.

All lenders require fire, theft, and liability insurance. Depending on where you live, the lender may also require other types of insurance. For example, if you live in a flood plain, you may require flood insurance.

# What Insurance Covers

When you purchase insurance on your home, you purchase a home owner's policy that includes two types of protection. **Casualty insurance** (also called *property protection* or *hazard insurance*) covers losses or damages to the home and contents caused by fire, theft, and certain weather-related hazards. **Personal liability** insurance protects you if you're sued by someone who's injured on your property. For example, if your Aunt Sunny has a few too many and falls off the porch, you're covered. Family members may also be covered if they're away from  home.

Your lender will require both types of coverage, but the extent of the coverage is up to you. You can select different types of insurance, as described next.

# How Much Do You Need?

When you're deciding how much coverage you need, consider a few things. First, ask your lender how much is required. The lender will require a minimum amount (usually purchase price less land value), but you may want to get additional coverage.

The amount of insurance you need (and the amount you pay) is based on the cost of replacing the entire structure and the value of your personal property. For example, you may have a $120,000 policy for replacement value and coverage of personal property up to $75,000.

You should insure your home for full replacement value. The current market value is what you can sell your home for today. The replacement value is the cost to replace your home.

To estimate the replacement costs, figure the square footage of floor space and then multiply this figure by the current construction

**Home Work**

A standard policy will not cover business assets. If you work from your home, you may need additional coverage.

cost per square foot for similar homes. You can find the construction cost by asking a local builder's association.

To cover your possessions, make an inventory. You can do this with pen and paper, a video camera, or a computer program. Once you determine a value for your possessions, find an appropriate insurance value. Keep in mind that there are certain monetary limits for specific items. For example, there may be a $1,000 limit on jewelry and furs or computer equipment. If you want additional insurance for specific items, you may have to pay more.

According to surveys, eight out of ten home owners carry too little insurance. Be sure you have enough coverage in case something happens. Also, update your insurance if the market changes, if the value of your possessions goes up or down, or if you make a major improvement to the home.

## Tips on Insurance

Shopping for insurance can be a headache. You should make sure you have enough coverage, that you keep your coverage up-to-date, and that you get the best bargain. Don't be tempted to save money by getting the least amount of coverage. This is your home! If you want to save money, don't scrimp on the policy. Instead, get a higher deductible. Doing so can lower the premium cost.

It's easy to put off getting insurance until the last minute. Then, since you need the policy at closing, you may just call Uncle Harry the broker or the first company you think of. It's better not to wait until the last minute. Shop around and get quotes from several companies. Rates can vary significantly from area to area and from company to company.

If you make a new purchase, keep your receipts and add the item to your inventory of possessions. Receipts will help if you have to file a claim.

Ask about discounts. You may get a discount from some insurers if you have both home and car insurance with the same company. Also, you may receive a discount if you have a smoke or burglar alarm or a newer home.

Check about changing the policy. Can you raise the coverage later? Some policies are tied to the Consumer Price Index and rise accordingly. You may have to pay extra for this feature.

Find out what isn't covered. If the pipe in your basement bursts and damages your belongings, is the damage covered? What about earthquakes (usually not covered)? Find out how damages are paid. You want the full replacement cost. If your roof is damaged, you want the insurer to cover the entire payment for a new roof — not a partial fee.

## How Payments Are Made

When you purchase a home, the lender usually requires that you pay for a one-year policy up front. You should ask your lender when the policy has to be delivered. Usually you must do so at or before closing. You'll most likely be asked to bring a paid receipt with the insurance policy.

## Getting Mortgage Insurance

Mortgage insurance is required by lenders if you get a high-ratio mortgage with a down payment of less than 25%. You'll have to pay about 0.5% to 2.5% of the total amount for mortgage insurance provided by the Canada Mortgage and Housing Corporation or the Mortgage Insurance Corporation of Canada. This guarantees the lender that the loan will be repaid even if you default. The premium is usually added proportionately to your monthly mortgage payment.

**Insured Mortgage vs. Mortgage Life Insurance**

Don't confuse this type of mortgage insurance with the kind that pays off the house if the owner dies. You'll be bombarded with offers for mortgage life insurance when you close on the house, starting with your lender. Usually there's a better and cheaper way to provide the same protection.

## Canceling Mortgage Insurance

Depending on the loan agreement, you may be able to cancel the insurance once you accumulate a certain amount of equity in your home. If your equity amounts to 25%, you may be able to stop paying insurance.

Check with the lender about how and when you can cancel. You have to request the cancellation in writing; the lender won't cancel automatically. The lender may require an appraisal if the property has been improved, a clean payment history (for instance, no more than a single late payment in 24 months), and a minimum payment history (for example, two years). Finally, you still have to occupy the property.

## The Least You Need to Know

Your lender considers himself a partner in your home. To protect his investment, he requires you to have several types of insurance.

➤ Your lender will require a certain amount of home owner's insurance. Don't get the minimum amount. Get enough to cover the replacement value of the home, plus your possessions.

➤ If you want to save money on your home owner's policy, don't scrimp on the coverage. Instead, get a higher deductible, shop around among insurers, and ask about any discounts.

➤ At or before the closing, you'll have to prove that you've purchased a one-year home owner's policy.

➤ If you have an insured mortgage or a high-ratio mortgage with less than 25% down, you'll have to pay mortgage insurance fees.

➤ In some cases, you can cancel your mortgage insurance once you build a certain level of equity in your home.

# Chapter 14

# Having the Home Inspected

| In this chapter |
| --- |
| ➤ Understanding seller disclosure |
| ➤ Scheduling an inspection |
| ➤ What the inspector checks |
| ➤ Reading the inspection report |
| ➤ Handling any problems |

Do you fear buying a house, moving in, and then finding a clan of termites eating your living room from the bottom up? Or finding out the roof is ready to cave in? Or turning on the shower and getting drenched in rust? You might think you looked carefully at the house before you made an offer, but even if you know everything there is to know about a house, you should hire a professional inspector to confirm or refute your impressions.

## Why Get an Inspection?

When you're adding up all the costs associated with buying a home, you may want to skimp on some fees. For example, you may want to ask

**Get a Sample**

Ask to see a sample report. By looking over the report, you can tell what the inspector usually inspects and how thoroughly he or she will inspect the home.

your Uncle Charlie to take a look at the house. Even though he sells mattresses now, he once built homes and knows a little about home construction. And he'll work for nothing.

Not a good idea.

Uncle Charlie's inspection is worth what you pay for it. You should hire a professional inspector and make your offer contingent on a satisfactory inspection.

An inspection can help you identify problems before you purchase a home. If there are problems, the inspection can persuade the sellers to make the necessary repairs, although it usually won't persuade them to adjust the price of the home. If the problems are big, the inspection report may enable you to withdraw your offer. If there aren't problems, the inspection will make you feel more secure in your decision to purchase the home.

# Organizing an Inspection

If you've made the offer conditional on an inspection, you usually have a certain period in which to schedule it. You should do it early so that you have time to review the findings and make changes, if necessary.

**The Good, the Bad, and the Ugly**

Of the approximately 5,000 home inspectors in Canada, fewer than 15% are registered with a self-governing organization. The rest are freewheeling, unregulated, and potentially fly-by-night operators.

You can find a good inspector by asking friends and relatives for referrals, by asking your real estate agent or lawyer, or by looking in the *Yellow Pages*. The Canada Mortgage and Housing Corporation (CMHC), which has initiated a program to regulate home inspectors, may also give you some useful information. In Ontario, the Ontario Association of Home Inspectors sets guidelines for members, who must have demonstrated experience in the field, six months' training, and malpractice insurance. There are similar organizations in other provinces.

When you find an inspector, ask about his training and qual[i]-tions, and ask for references. How long has he been in the business? What certification does he have?

Find out the cost for the inspection. Expect to pay from $250 to $500. You may also have to pay additional fees if you want certain tests done, such as a water test, radon test, or termite certification.

# What the Inspector Checks

A home inspector evaluates the condition of the property, including the wiring, plumbing, insulation, roof, basement, heating system, and foundation, then prepares a written report.

When the inspector schedules his visit, you should arrange to accompany him around the home. In fact, the inspector will encourage you to do this. As you follow him around the place, he can tell you what he's doing and what he's discovering. If you go along for the in-spection, you'll be in a better position to understand the written report. You can also ask questions and see how extensively the inspector looks at the house. He should crawl down in the crawlspace, get up on the roof, poke around in the insulation, turn on all the faucets, and more. Expect to spend about two hours on a home inspection.

# What the Inspector Should Check

At the minimum, the inspector should visually examine the following:

➤ **Foundation** Check for cracks and any separation in the foundation.

➤ **Doors and windows** Make sure all the windows and doors open and close properly.

➤ **Roofing, chimney, gutters, vents, and fans** Determine whether the gutters drain properly and are in good condition, and whether the roof system needs to be replaced or repaired.

➤ **Plumbing** Check drains, water pressure, water heater, leakage, etc.

➤ **Electrical system** Check wiring, fuses or circuit breakers, groundings, outlets and switches.

➤ **Heating and cooling systems** Check furnace, air conditioning, etc.

➤ **Ceilings, walls, and floors** Note any cracks, moisture prob-lems, or significantly uneven floors or walls.

➤ **Insulation and ventilation**  Is there enough insulation? Too much?

➤ **Septic tanks, wells, or sewer lines**  Usually, you get a separate report on septic and well water because the water must be tested for bacteria.

➤ **Exterior (decks, doors, windows)**  Check for signs of rot and determine whether the house needs repainting

➤ **Property**  Check garage, fences, paved areas, and other outside facilities as well as drainage.

➤ **Basement and attic**  Check for leaks and water damage.

In addition to the routine inspection, you can ask for other tests. For example, you may want to test for radon, lead paint, asbestos, hazardous waste, and other environmental concerns. You may be charged extra for these tests.

## What the Inspector Doesn't Check

The inspector doesn't check the cosmetic features of the home, such as the carpeting and wall coverings. Nor does the inspector provide a warranty that the home is free of problems. He simply reports on existing problems.

Most inspectors are generalists. If they uncover a problem, they may recommend a type of specialist who can fix it, although an inspector shouldn't make a specific referral. For instance, if the electricity is troublesome, the inspector may recommend having an electrician take a look. The inspector can also suggest a general price to pay for the repairs.

## What the Inspector Shouldn't Do

During the inspection, the inspector shouldn't tell you what the house is worth. Nor should he give you advice on whether you should buy the house. Finally, the inspector shouldn't offer to make repairs on the house himself and shouldn't refer you to anyone in particular to make the repairs, especially his brother.

## Reading the Inspection Report

After the inspector has flipped on all your light switches, crawled around in your attic, climbed up on the roof, and checked how well all your sinks drain, he will write an inspection report. This report will include general information about your property as well as information about the weather conditions when the inspection occurred.

Why include the weather conditions? If an inspector works during the middle of winter, he may not be able to check the air conditioning. In this case, he may make a note to do so later. Also, bad weather may prevent the inspector from examining a rooftop. In some cases, he may make a return trip to fully inspect the house. There's usually a charge for the return trip.

**Daylight Saving**

Be sure to schedule the inspection during the day. An evening inspection may be more convenient, but the inspector can take a better look at the home during the daylight hours.

The report will cover each element of the home, such as the basement, crawlspace, central heating, cooling, electrical system, plumbing system, interior structure, attic, doors and windows, garage, exterior structure, grounds, and appliances.

Usually the report includes a description of each system. For example, for an electrical system, the inspector may note amps and volts. The inspector may note whether the system is satisfactory, not applicable, or problematic.

# Handling Any Problems

If the inspection turns up any problems, which it most likely will, you'll need to decide whether you should address the problem prior to closing or after you move in. If your offer was conditional on inspection, you can handle problems in any of the following ways:

➤ If the problem is minor, you may choose to ignore it. For instance, you shouldn't have a fit if one window screen is missing or if the porch light doesn't work.

➤ If the problem is significant, you should point it out to the seller and negotiate a settlement. For example, if the home needs a new roof, you may ask the seller to contribute some or all of the cost.

➤ Instead of adjusting the price, you may ask the seller to make the repairs or to set aside money to have repairs done.

➤ If the problem is serious and materially affects the structure of the home, you can withdraw the offer. Usually, you must give the sellers a chance to make the repairs, though. But sellers and their agents are obligated to disclose any material facts about the home that affect its condition.

➤ Generally, you ask sellers to make repairs to items that affect habitability. The seller has the option of making the repairs or allowing you to withdraw your offer.

➤ If you conclude that the seller or his agent has grossly misrepresented the condition of the home, you should withdraw the offer.

# The Least You Need to Know

An inspection by a professional inspector is a must to reassure yourself that the house is free of problems. If it does have problems, you'll want to know about them before the closing. An inspection costs $250 to $500.

➤ When you make an offer, be sure to make it conditional on an inspection and state in the offer that the inspection must meet your satisfaction.

➤ To find an inspector, ask your lawyer, agent, or friends and relatives for a referral or contact your provincial home inspectors association.

➤ The inspector should check the foundation, doors, windows, roof, chimney, gutters, plumbing, electrical system, heating and cooling, ceilings, walls, floors, insulation, ventilation, septic tanks, wells, sewer lines, exterior of the house, and property.

➤ After the inspection, the inspector will give you a written report. If the inspection uncovers problems, you can choose to ignore the problem, ask the seller to fix the problem or, in extreme cases, withdraw the offer.

# Chapter 15

# Handling the Closing: Buyer's Point of View

## In this chapter

➤ Understanding what you must do before the closing
➤ Preparing for the closing costs
➤ Going to the closing
➤ Handling problems
➤ After the closing — moving in!

Finally! The big day has arrived. The last step in buying a home is the closing. At the closing, you'll sign document after document after document, turn over all your money, then get the much-anticipated keys to your new home. This chapter tells you what to expect at closing.

## What Has to Happen Before the Closing

Getting to the closing is a kind of race. You have to leap several hurdles before you cross the finish line. Here are the hurdles you can expect to jump.

First, you need financing. This topic is covered in Chapter 12. Unless you're paying cash for the home, you'll need a down payment, a

**Insure Early**

Don't wait until the last minute to get insurance or you may sign up with the first insurance company you find. It makes more sense to shop around and get several quotes so that you get the best deal.

mortgage loan, and a commitment letter from the lender. The commitment letter, which goes to your lawyer, verifies that you have the money to buy the house. You've jumped hurdle one.

Second, the lender will require that you insure the home. Before the closing, you'll need to arrange for insurance. Usually, you must show a one-year paid policy. Insurance is covered in Chapter 13.

Third, if you already own a home, you'll have to sell it. We cover selling your home later in this book.

Fourth, you or the seller may have to negotiate about repairs, appliances, or other issues before the closing.

The final two things that must be done — deciding how to hold the title and having the final walk-through — are described here.

## Who Owns the House?

As part of the closing, you'll be asked how you want to hold the title. Holding the title refers to the form of ownership. Do you own the house alone? Do you own it with a partner? How will you share the property shared? You determine the form of ownership by selecting how to hold the title. Here are the most common ways:

**Sole ownership** You are the only owner. If you're buying the home alone, you'll probably select this.

**Joint tenancy** Used when two or more people purchase a home. When one owner dies, the surviving owner automatically gets the deceased's share; the property does not become an asset to be passed on as part of the deceased's estate to the beneficiaries.

**Tenancy in common** Each party owns an equal share of the home. If one owner dies, his or her share goes to his or her heirs.

## The Final Walk-Through

As part of the purchase agreement, the seller agrees to turn the property over in the same condition as it was when you first saw it. If the house has been inspected and you've removed the inspection contingency, then you've agreed you're satisfied with the property. A final walk-through allows you to be sure that the owner has made no major changes since you last saw it. If there have been changes, the transaction can be opened up for renegotiation.

If you want a final walk-through, be sure to say so in your purchase contract. You should schedule the walk-through before the closing. Give yourself enough time to settle any problems that pop up. If you schedule the walk-through for the morning of the closing and find problems, you won't have time to resolve them.

During the final walk-through, check the major systems (electrical, plumbing, and so on) and check the appearance of the house.

Next, check the personal property in the house. Is property that's supposed to be there really there? For example, if you asked the sellers to leave the washer and dryer as part of the deal, are the washer and dryer still there? Are the curtains and other floor coverings still there? Is property that's supposed to be gone truly gone? For example, if the sellers had an old refrigerator in the basement that you wanted them to remove, did they take it? Or did they leave it for you to haul out? Any disputes about personal property should be addressed before you close.

# The Cost of Closing

Closing on a house can be exciting, because you'll soon have the keys to your new home. You'll also have an empty wallet, because you'll have to pay all the closing costs.

## Don't Forget the Down Payment

At the closing, you'll need to pay the balance of the down payment on the house. If you're buying a $100,000 home and putting 10% down, you must have $10,000 for the down payment. Some of this amount may come from your deposit. The rest will come from your own resources.

## Costs You Can Expect to Pay

In addition to the down payment, you'll have to pay closing costs. The following sections list the fees you can expect to pay at closing. Keep in mind that some closing costs may be paid by the seller, and some will be paid before closing. For example, you might have paid a loan application fee, which is considered a closing cost. This fee, though, is paid at the time of application.

## Items Payable in Connection with the Loan

**Assumption fee** If you are assuming a mortgage, you may have to pay an assumption fee. In a competitive market, however, the lender should waive this fee in return for getting your business.

**Application fee** When you apply for the loan, you may be charged an application fee. This fee may run up to $350, and is paid at the time of application. Again, in a competitive market, most lenders will waive this fee.

**Credit report** At the time of application, you may be asked to pay the fee for checking your credit history. This fee can run from $40 to $60. Sometimes this fee is included as part of the application fee.

**Appraisal fee** Paid at application, this fee runs from $225 to $300. You have to pay this fee, whether you like it or not.

**House inspection** To have the home inspected, you'll have to pay a professional inspector $250 to $500, usually at the time of the inspection. If the lender requires further tests — for pests, for example — after the inspection, you'll have to pay for these as well.

**Processing fees** The lender may charge you various fees for processing the loan. These fees may include a mail or delivery fee, a document preparation fee, an underwriting fee, and other fees. You can pay from $100 to $400 when all these fees are totaled, although you should try to find a lender who will forego them to win your business.

## Items Required by the Lender to be Paid in Advance

**Prepaid interest** Depending on when you close on your house, you may have to prepay the interest for the month.

**Mortgage insurance** If your loan requires mortgage insurance, you'll be required to pay for it at the time of closing, usually from the proceeds of your mortgage loan.

**Insurance** You'll have to buy a one-year prepaid policy on your home.

# Reserves Deposited with the Lender

**Mortgage insurance** You may have to pay a few months' worth of mortgage insurance, if it's required by your lender.

**Property taxes** You may have to set aside money for your property taxes with your lender. Lenders sometimes require borrowers to include monthly tax payments with their mortgage payments.

# The Title Search

The lender requires a title search, which you pay for, through your lawyer. In a title search, your lawyer searches all the records and traces the history of ownership, starting with the current seller and working backwards from owner to owner until the initial conveyance of the property.

A title search uncovers not only the succession of owners, but also reveals any unpaid taxes on the property, liens, easements, or encroachments. An easement is a permanent right to use another's property. For example, the phone company or other utility company may have an easement to put up phone lines or poles in your backyard. You may also have an easement if you share a driveway.

The title search also uncovers any encroachments. It makes sure that nothing of yours is actually on your neighbor's property, and that nothing of the neighbor's is on your property.

## Partly Cloudy, Chance of Thunderstorms

Someone in the title business must have been a frustrated meteorologist; that would explain all the weather terms. You want a clear title. If it's not clear, it has a cloud on it, which indicates a problem with the title. For example, any claims made against a property by a person or any tax assessment for payment of a debt could cloud a title.

If during the title search a cloud appears on the horizon, it has to be cleared up. Either the person with the claim can release the debt lien or sign a quit claim deed. A quit claim deed releases any right to the property. Or if there is a record-keeping error, it can be corrected. Your lawyer can advise you in more detail on your options if there's a cloud on the title.

## Title Charges

**Lawyer** Your lawyer will charge several hundred dollars, at a minimum, for conducting the title search, preparing the mortgage documents, and corresponding with the seller's lawyer, the lender, and you. It's well worth the cost.

## Additional Settlement Charges

**Survey** The lender will require an up-to-date survey to confirm that there are no encroachments on your property. The survey will cost $250 or more.

**Condo and co-op fees** You may be charged a move-in fee or association transfer fees.

**Adjustments** If the sellers prepaid their taxes for six months, but lived in the home for only three months, they'll ask for a three-month adjustment. They'll also ask for an adjustment on any utility bills they've prepaid.

**Land transfer tax** Provincial governments charge a tax for the

### When Is My House Payment Due?

Payments on a mortgage are made differently from rent payments. You pay mortgage payments in arrears. That means, for example, a payment made on September 1st covers the month of August, not September. When you close, you'll have to prepay for the remainder of the month that you close in. Then you'll skip a month and start paying on the house the following month.

privilege of buying a home, based on the purchase price of the property. The higher the price, the more you pay. It can range from 0.5% of the price to 4%.

**GST** On a new home, you have to pay GST, although you can receive a partial rebate if the home costs less than $350,000. The rebate reduces the effective tax rate to 4.5%.

## The Total Comes to...

Before the actual closing, the lender will tell your lawyer (who in turn will tell you) the precise amount of money you must bring to the closing. You have the right to review the settlement charges one business day before the closing. You often won't get much time to pore over the final figures, but the settlement statement and your lawyer will explain exactly which fees are paid and by whom.

When you meet at your lawyer's office on the day of closing, you'll need a certified cheque for the balance of the down payment and closing costs. Your lawyer will tell you in advance the exact amount you'll need.

> **Back and Forth**
>
> If you close on August 15, you have to prepay your mortgage interest for the remaining days in August (the 16th to the 31st, or 16 days). The payment for September is due October 1 and covers September 1 through 30. In essence, you skip a payment for September.

It's a good idea to have the cheque made out to yourself. You can then endorse the cheque at the closing.

## What Happens at Closing

You can think of a closing as an invitation to a big event. Here are the juicy details:

**Event:** Depending on the location, closing can be referred to as closing, settlement day, whatever. This is the big day, the final step in buying a home.

**When:** You determine the date of closing when you and the seller come to an agreement over the terms of the purchase and sale. Closing usually occurs one or two months after the agreement is made, but it can be adjusted.

**Where:** The closing is usually held at your lawyer's office.

**Occasion:** And finally, the reason for the closing: to sign papers and exchange money.

**The Fine Print**

There generally isn't time to read the documents entirely at closing. If you want to read them, ask to have them prepared and ready for you a day in advance.

## What You Should Bring to the Big Event

When you're preparing to attend the closing, you'll need your certified cheque, a home owner's insurance policy, and any other documentation required by the lender.

## Signed, Sealed, and Delivered

One of the main purposes of the closing is to review and sign all the appropriate documents. You should carefully look over each document you are asked to sign before signing. If you notice any discrepancies, you should bring them to the attention of your lawyer. You should also get a copy of every document.

During the closing, you can expect to review the following documents:

**Note** This is your promise to pay and the terms of your payment. The document includes the terms of the loan, date on which your payments must be made, location of payment, penalties assessed, and other loan information.

**Mortgage, or deed of trust** This document describes in detail your agreement with the lender. It usually gives the lender claim to your property if you default. The document restates the information in the mortgage note.

**Affidavits** Certain affidavits may be required by provincial law or the lender. For instance, you may have to sign an affidavit stating that you'll use the property as your primary residence.

**Title** The seller turns over property by means of a warranty deed. Sellers attest that they have not taken any new loans on the property.

The deed should be properly signed and notarized. The transfer of the deed will be recorded at the registry of deeds or clerk's office.

Your lawyer will also return all the other documents that you've gathered in the process of concluding the deal, such as your survey, tax returns, and other information.

# Exchanging Money

In addition to signing documents, you'll exchange money. You'll pay the amount you owe, and the sellers will receive the amount they are due. The agent will receive his commission, and the loan company will receive its money.

### The Redecorating Cycle

Be prepared for the redecorating cycle. When you move in, you'll find that the couch doesn't go with the carpet in the living room. When you recarpet, the recliner will look shabby, so you'll need a new one. While you're at it, you might as well pick out a new coffee table, but now the couch doesn't fit with the new carpet, recliner, and coffee table. After you paint the room to go with the new couch, carpet, recliner, and coffee table, the dining room will need work. Rest assured that one day everything will be perfect. That's the day you put the "For Sale" sign up and hope to recoup all your redecorating dollars.

# The Passing of the Keys

After all the documents have been signed and all the money exchanged, you are finally the proud owner of the home. However, the seller's lawyer will still have to deliver the keys to the home to your lawyer. This may happen promptly; it may happen after a short delay; or you may sit around twiddling your thumbs for hours, waiting for the keys to arrive so you can move into your new home. Don't make any plans based on your expectations of the keys' arrival. It will likely not happen according to your schedule.

### Head 'em Up, Move 'em Out

The closing of your transaction will occur at any time of the day. It may happen in the morning. It may happen in the afternoon. It may happen in the evening. It depends on the lawyers, the lenders, and all sorts of other little gremlins that you'll never see but who can sabotage your exquisite timing. With this in mind, don't book a moving company to load up the truck and start shifting your furniture to your new home at the crack of dawn. The truck, the movers, and you will likely end up sitting in the driveway of your new home for six or seven hours, waiting for the keys to arrive at your lawyer's office. The movers won't mind. They get paid for their time. And the payment comes out of your pocket.

Nevertheless, when you do receive all the keys to the house, the place is yours. Congratulations!

# Handling Problems

The closing is a hectic time for all involved. The seller is getting ready to move. The lender has to organize all the appropriate paperwork for the loan package. You have to gather your money and prepare to move as well. Problems, both minor and major, can occur. This section describes some problems you might encounter.

## Walk-Through Problems

If you conduct a final walk-through and find a problem, you'll need to decide how to handle it. If the problem is a minor one, you may decide to ignore it. If the problem is major, your response will depend on whether or not it was disclosed at the time of the sale. If the seller told you that the basement leaks, and you walk through and see water, you don't have much recourse. If the seller didn't tell you the basement leaks, and it's flooded, you should call your agent and your lawyer, if necessary, and have the problem fixed. You may have legal recourse.

**What the...!**

Be sure to get any mailbox keys or garage door openers. The seller may forget these items, but you'll need them when you go to pick up your mail or park your car.

## Money Problems

With all the number crunching, the numbers still may not add up. For example, you may owe more than you originally thought. Your lawyer should have prepared you for the total closing costs at the time of application.

## Loan Problems

For the closing to take place, you need the loan package — the documents that spell out the terms of the loan. Without these documents, you can't close on the home. If the documents are late, the lender will send them by courier. (Guess who pays for that? You.)

You have to clear up any inaccuracies before the closing. For example, if the loan documents say you're paying 8.75% interest, but you'd agreed to pay 8.5% interest and can prove it, the error must be corrected.

You don't close on a house very often, so the charges may seem confusing. Your lawyer is much more familiar with this part of the transaction. Be sure that he goes over the final charges in advance and agrees with them.

## Title Problems

Remember that the title is your evidence that you own the house. To be sure the seller has the right to grant that title freely, your lawyer has conducted a title search. If a title problem occurs before the closing, it must be cleared up before you close.

# Timing Problems

If they already own a home and sell it before moving, most people try to coordinate the closing of the purchase with the closing of the sale. If this works, then you simply hand over the keys to your current house to the new owners, and retrieve the keys to your new home from the sellers.

If this doesn't work — and it often doesn't — there will be a period between the sale of your home and the purchase of your new one. Or you may close on the purchase before you close on the sale. One way or the other, you'll have to make arrangements for this interim period.

If you sell your home before you close on the purchase of your new one, then you can arrange to move temporarily or see if the purchaser will let you remain in the home until your other deal closes.

If you close on the purchase before you close on the sale, you'll have to come up with the money to pay for the new home before you receive any money from the sale of your current home. This requires financing, and unless you have rich parents, it usually takes the form of a bridge loan. For two weeks or two months — whatever the period required — a lender will provide you with the money necessary to close on the deal for your new home while you wait for the deal to close on your current home. But if you already have a mortgage on your current home, the lender will need security in some other form as reassurance that you'll repay the bridge loan. Otherwise, there's nothing to stop you from taking the unsecured bridge loan and moving to Peru.

This can get complicated, and may even scuttle your entire deal. You might need a guarantee from a parent; perhaps your lawyer can help. One way or the other, though, you'll need that bridge loan. And you'll have to pay for it too.

## The Law of Expanding Possessions

If you're moving from a small house to a larger house, be prepared for the Law of Expanding Possessions: if you have a two-bedroom house full of junk and move to a four-bedroom house, you'll soon have a four-bedroom house full of junk.

# Moving In!

At the end of the entire home-buying process, you may find yourself exhausted. So much has to be done before you get your dream house. So many problems, big and small, can make the entire process tense. Your satisfaction will come when you can finally move in. The dream of owning a home is then yours! Here are a few tips on getting ready for the move:

*Don't take everything with you.* Have a garage sale or give items away to charity. Moving is a great time to get rid of possessions you don't need or don't use.

*Start saving newspapers and boxes* as soon as you know that you will be moving. You can use them when you pack your stuff.

*If possible, do your redecorating before you move in.* Painting or wallpapering a room that's full of furniture is more difficult than painting or wallpapering an empty room.

*Put the utilities in your name.* You should contact the phone company, gas company, electric company, water company, garbage collection company, recycling company, and any other utilities or services to put the service in your name. Likewise, discontinue the utilities at your old residence.

*Fill out a change-of-address card.* Be sure to let the post office know your new address, and to send address-change postcards to friends, family, businesses, magazines, etc.

*Meet the neighbors.* As you move in, your neighbors will see the moving trucks and be curious. Now's a great time to say hello and get to know your new neighbors.

*Start a house file.* In this file, keep all the documents pertaining to the purchase of your home. Also, keep a record of home improvements.

# The Least You Need to Know

Closing on the home is the final step in the purchase. At this event, you sign the appropriate documents, exchange money, and get the keys to your new home.

➤ Before the closing, you need a loan approval, a one-year insurance policy, and other documents specified by your lender.

➤ If you include it in your offer to purchase, you can take a final walk through the house to make sure it's in the same condition as it was when you made the offer. If you want a final walk-through, be sure to put it in the contract.

➤ At the closing, you must pay the remaining amount of the down payment. You should also be prepared to pay closing costs, which can amount to 2% of the purchase price. Your lawyer will tell you the exact amount you need to bring. You'll need a certified cheque to cover the full amount.

➤ The closing occurs at the time specified in your purchase agreement. It may be held at your lawyer's office or someplace else, depending on local custom.

➤ At the closing, you can expect to sign the mortgage affidavits, disclosures, and any other forms required by the lender.

# Part IV
# Sell Your House

*There are some people who buy one home and never leave again. They never have to worry about the prospect of selling, because they never intend to sell. Other people think they won't move, but they do. In fact, most people stay in their homes an average of five to seven years. That means that, just when you finish all your remodeling projects, just when the house is exactly the way you want it to be, the time comes to move on. A word of caution on those remodeling projects, though: be careful not to make your house look too eccentric. Remember, beauty is in the eye of the beholder.*

# Chapter 16

# Deciding to Sell Your Home

## In this chapter

➤ Understanding why you want to sell

➤ Timing the sale

➤ Understanding the costs involved in selling your home

➤ Knowing what to expect

If you're reading this section, you've probably already endured the joys of being a home buyer and a home owner; now you're preparing for the delights available only to the home seller. Dozens of muddy-footed strangers trudging through your home, criticizing your wallpaper, your bathrooms, your kitchen cabinets, your wedding portrait. Weeks spent cleaning, polishing, repairing, 'till the house looks so good you may wonder why you're moving.

Why are you moving, anyway? Are you tired of standing in line outside the only bathroom in the house, waiting for your turn to shower and shave every morning? Tired of hearing your teenage daughter complain about having to share a bedroom with her four-year-old brother? Maybe you work in the attic, where the single electrical outlet can't handle your computer, fax, modem, desk lamp, and copier. Or maybe you love your current residence but are being transferred to a new city and must move.

No matter what the reason, you've decided to sell your house. You might just stick a FOR SALE sign in the yard and hope for the best. But the best will take a long time to come. Selling a home properly takes a lot of preparation. This chapter helps with the initial decision: do you really want to sell?

# Why Do You Want to Sell?

Most people decide to sell their home because they find another one they like better. This may happen for many reasons. The new home might be across the street, around the corner, across the city, or in another country. Perhaps they grew tired of their current home, perhaps they were transferred. Perhaps they needed more room. Whatever the reason, most people find a new home before they sell their current one.

Before you decide to put that for-sale sign up and move on, you should take a careful look at why you want to move. It's easy to put your house on the market for the wrong reason. To avoid making a mistake, ask yourself why you want to sell.

If you have to move because of your job, you may not have to look into your motivation much further. If you're moving simply because you want a new house or because you think you'll make a potful of money from the sale of your current one, or because your current neighbors drive you nuts by playing the tuba all night, you may not have a good enough reason to move. Why do you want a new house?

## Likes, Dislikes, Wishes, and Wants

Before you decide to pack up and move to a new house, be sure you aren't packing up your troubles and moving them with you. Maybe it's really your furniture that you hate. Maybe you love the house, but just need a few changes. Maybe you have an obsessive personality and get disturbed by the sound of grass growing. Before you make a radical decision to move, it's a good idea to analyze what you like and dislike about your house.

What do you dislike about the home? If you're frustrated with your home, you can easily make a list of what you dislike. For example, suppose that it's July 1, 104° F outside, and you don't have central air conditioning. You may hate the house because it's hot.

After you make a list of what you don't like, look over your list and then note whether you can change any of the dislikes into likes. For example, if you could change the house, what would be different? Would you have more bedrooms? Central air? A bigger yard?

Some changes aren't possible. If you hate the location of the house, you simply can't change that. If changes are possible — for instance, installing central air — consider the cost.

Next make a list of what you like about the house. Perhaps it has a nice view or you like the neighborhood. Maybe the house has built-in cabinets that you enjoy. Perhaps you like more than you think.

Once you have a more specific idea of what you like and dislike, you can take a better look at why you want to move. If you love the location, but simply need more room, you may want to add a room rather than move. Or maybe you just need some redecorating or new furniture.

On the other hand, if the house can't be redone to suit your needs, you'll know you really do want to move. You'll also have a better understanding of what to look for in your next home.

### Like It, Like It, Hate It...

You can use your list of likes and dislikes when you're shopping for a new home. Defining your dream home is covered in Chapter 5.

## What Do You Hope to Gain?

In addition to reviewing the home's pluses and minuses, ask yourself what you hope to gain by moving. You may answer: a bigger home, more money, fewer commitments. Knowing what you hope to gain can help you plan your strategy.

Ask yourself how realistic your goals are. For example, suppose that the real estate market is hot and you want to sell now so that you can make a profit. Making money is the primary reason you're selling. In this case, keep in mind that you still need someplace to live. If you sell in a seller's market, you'll likely have to buy in a seller's market. Will you really gain anything? Also, consider the time, energy, and money involved in selling. Is the gain worth the pain? (Later in this chapter, the section "What Costs Are Involved?" discusses the costs involved in selling a home.)

As another example, suppose you have a large house, your children are grown and have moved out, and you're retiring. You want to sell your house and buy a condominium so that you don't have to incur the expense and effort of maintaining a large home. You want to sell your home to another family who will enjoy the pleasures of your home. Your motivation here is a release from current commitments.

If you can verbalize your reasons, you can better plan when to sell and what to emphasize when you do it.

# Timing the Sale

Timing the sale of your home depends on many factors. First you have to make up your mind that you're ready to sell. Then, in most cases, you have to coordinate the sale of your current home with the purchase of a new residence. This section discusses these timing issues.

## When Is the Best Time to Sell?

There are no pat answers for this question. The best time to sell is when you're ready to sell. Many things can affect your readiness to sell.

One is your job. If you're being transferred, you may want to put your house on the market right away. If you live in a two-bedroom house and are about to have your second child, you may be ready to move to a bigger home, but you don't have to move immediately. If you're divorcing, you may want to sell the house as soon as possible. If you're taking in an elderly parent, you may be ready to look for a more accommodating house. If your last child has just moved out, you may not need the big four-bedroom home and may be ready for a smaller house.

The economy is another factor. If interest rates are sky high, you may have to stay in your current home, even if it doesn't meet your needs. If interest rates are low, you may be able to take advantage of the situation and trade up to a more expensive home as an alternative to refinancing.

Another good time to move up is in a buyer's market. You may have to sell your current home at a lower price, but you'll be in a stronger position to buy a more expensive house, especially if you've accumulated some equity in your home.

Only you can determine your timing to move. But when you're ready to move, you're ready to sell.

# Buying Your Next Home

Timing the sale of your home with the purchase of a new home can be tricky. Should you buy first and then sell? Or should you buy and sell at the same time? Or should you sell and then buy? Each of these has its strengths and weaknesses.

# Buy First

If you find your next house first and then purchase it, you know you have somewhere to live. You don't have to worry about being forced to find a house after you sell yours.

On the other hand, this strategy is risky. For one thing, you have to come up with a down payment on the new house. If you have ready cash, that may not be a problem. But if you're counting on the proceeds from your current home to cover the cost, it might be.

You could end up with two houses and two mortgage payments. To avoid doubling up on the mortgages, you can make the purchase of your new house conditional upon the sale of your existing house. Sellers don't usually like such conditions and, in a sellers' market, they don't have to accept it. After all, they don't know anything about your home. What if it's a dump and you never get rid of it? They may not want to tie up their property while yours is on the market, and they may reject your offer.

Or the sellers may limit your condition. For example, they may continue to keep their house on the market. If they get another offer, you have the right to remove your condition and buy the house or withdraw your offer.

This approach also puts pressure on you to sell. You may accept an offer that you wouldn't have accepted if you weren't under the gun.

## Buy and Sell Together

Most people put their home on the market and begin looking for a new home at the same time. This strategy can work perfectly: you could close on your current home and your new home on the same day.

## Sell First

Some sellers choose to sell their home first. This puts them in a strong bargaining position. First, they don't have to include a condition for selling their home. Second, they know how much money they've made (or lost) from the sale of their first home.

The danger in this strategy is that you might end up with nowhere to live. If your new buyers want to move in and you haven't found another home, you may end up living in an apartment or with relatives for awhile.

# What Costs Are Involved?

There are many costs involved in selling:

*Repair expenses.* As you get your home ready, you may find that you have to make certain repairs. You can do some of them yourself or you can hire someone to complete them. Deciding which repairs to make is covered in Chapter 17.

Even if you think the house is in perfect condition, the buyer will likely have your home professionally inspected. If the inspection turns up problems, you may have to pay for repairs.

*Sales commission.* If you list your house with an agent, you pay the agent's commission — usually 6% of the selling price. Negotiating commissions and selecting an agent is covered in Chapter 18. If you sell the home yourself, you don't pay the commission. Selling your home yourself is covered in Chapter 22.

*Closing costs that you must pay.* Some closing costs are customarily paid by the seller.

*Closing costs that you offer to pay.* As part of the negotiating process, you may offer to pay additional closing costs for the buyer. Deciding what you want to offer is covered in Chapter 19.

*Moving expenses.* Unless you have one duffel bag of stuff, moving your entire home is going to cost some money — even if you do it yourself. You'll have to hire a moving company or rent a moving truck.

*Costs for buying a new home.* If you're buying a new home after selling your current one, don't forget to plan for the costs involved in buying a home. Chapter 2 gives a preview of the costs you can expect to pay.

# What to Expect When You Sell Your Home

The remaining chapters discuss all the aspects of selling a home. This section is intended to give you a preview of what to expect.

## Step 1: Getting the House Ready

When you decide to sell your home, you need to get it ready. You need to decide what repairs to make and what information to collect.

As you get your house ready, expect to "undecorate." This advice is usually surprising to first-time sellers. "What? Put away all my family portraits? But that's what makes the home look like a home! Paint all the walls white? Where's the character in that?" The reason you want to undecorate your home and other strategies for getting ready are covered in Chapter 17.

## Step 2: Deciding Whether to Use an Agent

Deciding whether to sell your home yourself or through an agent is an important decision. You may be tempted to stick a FOR SALE sign in the front yard, sit back, and save the 6% commission. But are you prepared to sit around and wait for a buyer? Are you prepared for the negotiating and haggling that must be done once you find one? Most buyers will expect you to share your savings with them. Chapter 18 covers the benefits of using an agent and explains how to select one.

But what if you're in a strong seller's market? If you notice a lot of FOR SALE signs going up and down quickly, chances are you can make out just fine without an agent. Chapter 18 covers the benefits and liabilities of selling your home yourself, and Chapter 22 teaches you how to do it.

## Step 3: Pricing and Marketing the House

Setting the price for your house can be tricky. The price will depend on the current market, what your house has to offer, and how quickly you want to sell. Your agent can help you come up with the listing price. Pricing is covered in Chapter 19.

In addition to pricing, you should work on marketing the home — getting buyers to notice your home over all the other homes for sale in the area. If you have an agent, he'll do most of the marketing, as covered in Chapter 19. If you're selling the home yourself, Chapter 22 includes marketing ideas.

You can also expect that, just when you sit down to a wonderful dinner, your agent will call and ask to bring a potential buyer through your home. You'll have to put the food in the oven and drive around the block for 30 to 45 minutes. Expect to waste a lot of time driving around the block or sitting in the local McDonald's while potential buyers tour your home.

Also, expect criticism. You may love the red velvet wallpaper in the bathroom, but expect to hear criticism of that and every other aspect of the house. Don't let the criticism weigh you down. One person may hate the wallpaper; another one may come along who loves it as much as you do.

## Step 4: Negotiating Offers

If you're lucky, you'll receive several offers on your house and you can pretty much dictate the terms. In most cases, though, you'll have to negotiate the terms. Negotiating means a little give and a little take. Your agent can help you negotiate offers; this topic is covered in Chapter 20.

## Step 5: Closing on the House

Once you accept an offer and the buyer has done his job (getting financing, for example), you're ready to close on the house, take your money and hand over the keys. Closing is covered in Chapter 21.

## Step 6: Buying a New House

Unless you're moving to an apartment, closing on the house is not the end of the process. Usually you'll buy a new house at the same time or soon after you sell your current house. In this case, it's back to square one, Chapter 1, to learn all you ever wanted to know about buying a house.

# The Least You Need to Know

Before you decide to put your home on the market, examine your reasons for doing so.

➤ Ask yourself what you like and dislike about your home. There are a lot of costs involved with selling. If you love the location, but just need more room, you may decide to add a room instead of moving.

➤ Examine your motivation for selling the home. What do you hope to gain? A better home? Money? Less commitment? Knowing what you hope to gain can help you plan your selling strategy.

➤ The best time to sell is when you're ready to sell. Readiness is affected by your family situation, your job, the economy, and other factors.

➤ Be prepared for the costs involved in selling your home — the sales commission, closing costs, moving expenses, repair expenses, plus the cost of buying a new home.

**Lots of fellows think a home is only good to borrow money on.**

—Kin Hubbard

# Chapter 17

# Getting the House Ready

## In this chapter

➤ Doing repairs

➤ Cleaning up

➤ Uncluttering the house

➤ Collecting pertinent information

➤ Understanding seller disclosure

Once you decide to put your house on the market, you have to get it ready. If your home's in perfect condition, this may involve a little straightening up. If your home is like most, though, you may need to do some repairs. Got a leaky faucet? Better fix it. Roof need repair? You can have it repaired or take the repairs into consideration when you price the house.

In addition to cleaning and repairing, you should start to collect the information you'll need to sell the house. Buyers will want to know about maintenance and upkeep. For example, what's the monthly electric bill? When was the furnace last checked? This chapter helps you prepare for the sale of your home.

### Inspect It Yourself

If you want to be super-prepared, you can hire a professional home inspector to identify any major adjustments you need to make before the buyer's inspector shows up. You can also provide a copy of the inspection report to potential buyers.

# Doing Repairs

There are several types of do-it-yourselfers. There's the ideal Mr. and Ms. Fixit who love to work on the home, do a perfect job, and finish all the work they start. On the far end of the scale, there's the handyman who's not handy at all, takes one look at a leaky faucet, and calls the plumber. If either of these descriptions fits you or your spouse, you're lucky — for the most part you won't have problems with the repairs.

Unfortunately, many of us fall somewhere in between. We can do the work, but we get bored silly or preoccupied just as we have the sink ripped out and the taps on the floor. Sometimes we do even more damage than we had on our hands when we began. So we hire someone to clean up, usually for twice as much money as we might have paid if we'd called him to begin with.

This section helps you decide what repairs to make.

## Inspecting the House

To start, you should do a thorough inspection of your house. Look through each room as if you were a buyer. What problems do you see? What sticks out? If you were a buyer, what would you notice? Note any problems on a piece of paper.

You may be tempted to ignore some problems. For example, you may think that the buyer won't notice the missing tile in the bathroom or that you can cover it up with a frilly pink bath mat. But if you noticed it, the buyer will notice it. Put the problem on your list.

Once you have a complete list of problems, you can decide what to fix yourself, what to hire someone to fix, and what you can let go. Here are some areas to check:

*Check all your floors.* Do you have any missing tiles? Are the baseboards in good shape? Do they need to be cleaned? Does the floor creak? Check the stairs for loose handrails.

*Check all the walls and ceilings.* Are the paint and wallpaper in good shape? Do holes or cracks need to be fixed? Do rooms need to be repainted? Is the wallpaper peeling in spots? Have your children glued posters on the walls?

*Check all the doors and windows.* Do they open smoothly? Do they shut completely? Any doorknobs missing? Any loose hinges? Are the windows caulked? Any broken or cracked panes? You could combine checking and cleaning in one process and wash the windows as you check. Clean windows make a good impression. Repair any broken doors or windows.

*Inspect the bathrooms.* Are the tiles clean and caulked? Any missing tiles? Do the faucets leak? You should replace damaged tiles in the kitchen and bath and fix any leaking faucets. Does the toilet flush properly? Are the walls clean and in good repair? Does the bathroom need to be painted or wallpapered? Check the water pressure. Make sure the water drains properly.

*Take a close look at your kitchen.* Do all the appliances work? Is the floor clean and free of missing tiles or cracked linoleum? What about the cabinets? Paint or wallpaper? What about the sink? Does it drain okay? Any leaks?

*Examine your basement or attic.* Clean out stored stuff (see "Eliminating Clutter," later in this chapter). In the basement, check pipes for leaks and check for any sign of dampness.

*Make sure the electrical system is in good shape.* Do you have any outlets that don't work? Any broken switches?

*Check the heating and cooling systems.* Make any necessary repairs.

### Neutral Is Us

If you have to repaint or repaper, select a neutral color. White or off-white are good choices. They may not do much to set off your tiger-striped couch, zebra chairs, and beaded doorways, but not everyone will have your tastes. It's better to stick with something neutral.

### Knobs and Dabs

A quick coat of paint on painted cabinets will make the entire kitchen brighter. Also, new knobs on the cabinets go a long way to update a kitchen.

**Big Problems**

A U.S. survey of home inspectors came up with the following list of sale-killing problems:

➤ Water in the basement or crawlspace

➤ Bad wiring

➤ Damaged roofs

➤ Heating system problems

➤ Poor overall maintenance (untrimmed shrubs, loose doors, dirty paint).

You may not notice these problems, but an inspector will. So fix them before they turn away prospective buyers.

Replace dirty air filters. You may have the heating and cooling systems professionally serviced.

*Check the roof, gutters, exterior walls, driveway, garage, and yard.* Does the roof need repairs? If so, make them. Does the outside need to be painted? Is the yard in good shape? Check for overgrown bushes, tree limbs touching roof, gutters. Repair any missing siding.

Your inspection tour may depress you. You may see problems that you never noticed before. Don't fret. Distinguish cleaning tasks from repair tasks that you can do, repair tasks you need to hire someone to do, and repairs you can ignore.

You'll uncover some problems on your inspection tour that are simply cleaning tasks. No one likes to scrub the bathroom floor until it shines, but maybe that's all it needs. Mark all the cleaning tasks and save them for later. Cleaning is covered in the next section. This section focuses on repairs.

## Deciding What Repairs to Make

As you review the repairs on your list, first decide which ones you really need to make. If you notice, for instance, that the roof needs repair, you can choose to have it repaired and pay for the new roof. Or you may note that the roof needs to be repaired and then price the house accordingly. If you don't have the money to repair it, you may choose the second approach and lower your selling price. In either case, you'll need estimates for the repair so that you can proceed or adjust the price accordingly.

## Do It Yourself or Hire Someone?

Once you decide to make the repair, are you going to do it yourself or hire someone? Some repairs are easy. Most people can paint, for example. Other repairs are harder and require a professional touch. If you need to rewire outlets, you'll probably need an electrician.

Be realistic when deciding what you can and can't do. You may want to save money by doing the repairs yourself, but if you don't have the time or talent, hire someone. You'll save money in the long run. You'll also avoid potential disputes with your mate. Life's too short to argue over a leaky faucet. Besides, if you're moving, you'll have enough to argue about.

> **Biggest Bang for the Buck**
>
> The most cost-effective improvements are to the kitchen and bathroom. If you convert a one-bathroom house to a two-bathroom house, you'll expand your market of possible buyers.

Most people overestimate the costs of minor repairs; they may not be as expensive as you think.

## Should You Remodel?

When you think about the repairs in your home, don't get carried away with remodeling. For example, you may want to redo the entire bathroom. Keep in mind a few cautions.

It's hard to recover your investment in extensive remodeling and renovations. You may think that adding a deck will add a huge value to your home, but that's unlikely.

Kitchen remodeling, however, does add value.

In general, though, it's better to leave the remodeling to the buyer if you know you'll likely sell your home.

If you move, you won't enjoy any of the benefits of the remodeling. You may have dreamed of a greenhouse, but now you'll never get to enjoy it. And potential buyers may not share your enthusiasm for gardening.

It's also a mistake to think that you can make even more money by fixing up the house. Likely, there's a top price for a house with your amenities and in your location. You may get this top price, but you'll most likely get no more than that, no matter how much you spend on renovations.

You should consider making changes if you have eccentric decor. Most buyers aren't very imaginative. They have difficulty seeing past the decor of a home. If they hate the red velvet wallpaper, they may ignore the entire house, without realizing they can easily recover the walls. If you have any out-of-the-ordinary decorating touches, you should subdue or eliminate them. Eccentricity is endearing but it doesn't sell homes.

### Cleaning Pro

Hire professional cleaners to do the initial, thorough scrubdown. This will ensure that the house is in tip-top condition. If a house looks well-kept and clean, buyers are more apt to think it has been well maintained.

# Cleaning Up

Cleaning your home in preparation for selling it is an ongoing process. First, you need to do a deep clean. Then you need to keep the house tidy so that when a potential buyer stops by you don't have to run around sweeping and dusting and mopping. This section covers the deep clean.

## First Impressions Count: Clean Up the Outside

Start with the outside. Stand back on the curb and take a look at your house. What do you notice? Are the hedges neat? Is the lawn overgrown? What's the first impression you get from the house?

The first impression of the house makes a big impact on the buyer. Even if they find their dream home inside, buyers will remember driving up to the place and seeing your dangling shutters and scruffy shrubbery. They'll remember trudging through the knee-high grass to

### Nice Buds

Flowers make the outside and inside of your home look inviting. If you're selling during the spring, plant flowers to make the yard look colorful and pleasant. You can plant them in the yard or in flower boxes. A pretty wreath on the door and a welcome mat are nice touches too.

get to the door, and tugging at the door as it scrapes across the porch. Therefore, you should make the home look and feel as inviting as possible from the outside.

Trim the hedges. Mow the lawn. Weed the walk. Plant flowers. Get rid of dead trees. Shovel the walk in the winter, rake the yard in the fall.

Also, repair any problems (such as an ill-fitting door) that you uncover in your home inspection. If you repair your roof, be sure to repaint the damaged ceilings.

## Cleaning the Inside

Now put away your hedge trimmers and lawn mower and get your mop, broom, bucket, and other supplies. It's time to start on the inside. Start with one room and clean it so that it passes the white-glove mother-in-law test. Don't just do your normal once-over with the feather duster; really clean. Scrub the cabinets, wash the baseboards, remove all the stuff from the shelves and dust them, clean the walls.

Shampoo the carpets or have them professionally cleaned. Wash the drapes. Clean the walls, floors, and ceilings. Every room should sparkle when you finish it. Then on to the next room, and the next room, and the next room.

## Eliminating Clutter

When buyers walk into your home, you don't want them to ogle your collection of Amish cross-stitch samplers. You want them to move into your house in their imaginations and wonder where they'll put their furniture. So you need to do two things. First, get rid of any clutter. Second, depersonalize the house. It shouldn't look lived in.

## Put Everything Away!

The kitchen is the worst clutter culprit. You may have all your appliances on the counter, baskets of stuff on the table, little Mikey's artwork on the refrigerator, cookbooks on the shelves, coupons on the window sills. Get rid of all of it! Yep, put everything away. All surfaces should be clean and clear, including the kitchen desk, if you have one. Clutter makes the buyer think the house is too small and doesn't have enough storage. Reducing the clutter will make the house look cleaner and more spacious — more room for those buyers to move in their own artwork, cookbooks, and appliances.

You should unclutter each and every room in the house. You may be so used to it that it's invisible to your eye, so have someone such as your agent point it out to you.

Also, unclutter places where clutter breeds — the basement, the attic, the garage, the storage closets. The basement is supposed to be a spot for clutter, but that doesn't mean you have to keep it that way. Now's a good time to take a look at all your possessions and get rid of stuff you don't need and don't use.

You'll find lots of excuses not to get rid of stuff. "I'm going to lose 50 pounds and wear this dress again." "I've never used that wine-making kit in the five years I've had it, but this year I'm going to make some Beaujolais!" "The coffee maker is fine; it just needs to be fixed." Will you really ever be able to wear those pants that you wore in your first year in high school?

Be ruthless! If it doesn't fit, throw it out. If you haven't used it in the last year, throw it out. If it doesn't work, throw it out.

Do something worthwhile with your clutter. Have a garage sale; donate it to charity; give it to Goodwill or the Salvation Army. Also, re-cycle old magazines and newspapers. Nursing homes, women's shelters, and so on use old magazines; those you can't give away, put in the recycling bin. Why not let someone else enjoy those possessions that you've hoarded for so long in your cluttered home?

You can't unclutter by shoving everything in a drawer or cabinet, because buyers like to peek in the drawers and cabinets. If you want to keep old books, photo albums, or baby clothes, pack the stuff away

### Safekeeping

Be sure to put your valuables someplace safe. Most of the time, an agent will escort potential buyers through your home, but don't leave money or jewelry out in the open or even in a drawer that someone can open quickly and unseen.

neatly. If necessary, store it in a commercial storage area or a friend's house.

And don't hide your valuables in a drawer or cabinet, either. They may disappear.

You should also get rid of old furniture, especially if you have a lot. Consider rearranging the furniture so that a room looks roomier. The house should look spacious.

## Undecorating the House

Okay. You've disposed of the clutter. Almost. Now you need to be brutal. You need to declutter even more — get rid of things you may not think of as clutter. You want the buyer to focus on the house, not on how cute you have it decorated.

*Put away your family photos.* You want buyers to imagine their family pictures on the mantel, not yours.

*Put away knickknacks and other collectibles.* You aren't striving for a house that looks lived in, but one that looks ready to be lived in.

## Collecting Information

The buyer will be interested not only in how the house looks but also in the maintenance and upkeep of the house. Collect the following information:

*Property tax statements.* Know how much you pay for property tax as well as when and how you pay. If you've prepaid for the next six months and then sell the house, you may ask for a proration of the taxes.

*Utility bills.* The buyer will want to know approximately what it costs to heat the house, how much you pay for electricity, how much you pay for water and sewage. Collect a few months' utility bills for each service and have this information available.

*Warranties.* If you're leaving your appliances, collect all warranties for them. If you have a new stove, the buyer will need the warranty information. You'll also want any warranties on repairs done on the home — for instance, if you redid the roof. If you live in a new house, the builder's warranty may still be effective, and in many cases, you can transfer it to a new owner.

**Tell the Truth**

If a potential buyer or agent asks a direct question, you must answer truthfully or be subject to a lawsuit. Don't tell them the crooked chimney is just a decoration if it actually leads to the furnace.

*Maintenance information.* It's a good idea to keep a record of the maintenance you've done on the home. A record indicates to the buyer that you've kept track of the maintenance. For example, a buyer may want to know when you had the heating system serviced, the chimney cleaned, and so on.

## Disclosing Bad News

In disclosing information about your house, you're not providing a warranty. You're not saying the water heater won't break, you're saying it works now and you don't know of any problem. Also, you don't necessarily have to fix any problems; you just have to let the seller know about them if they could affect the home's value.

If you want to be fully prepared for all problems, have the home inspected. An inspector can spot problems more easily than you. Also, an inspector allows you to defer the blame. You can point your finger at the inspector if a problem turns up later unexpectedly.

## The Least You Need to Know

Getting your home ready for the market will involve first inspecting the home through the buyer's eyes and then doing any needed repairs and clean-up.

➤ Thoroughly examine every room and all major systems of your home and note any problems. Check for any sale-killing problems such as water in the basement, bad wiring, damaged roof, or heating problems.

➤ If you're planning extensive remodeling, keep in mind that it's hard to recover that money. Buyers will consider the value of other homes in the area. If you have the only $200,000 home in a $115,000 area, you may not recover the price you've spent.

➤ Clean up the outside and the inside of your home. A clean, clutter-free home looks bright and spacious. As buyers tour your home, they should imagine their own furnishings in it, not trip over yours.

➤ To prepare for the sale of your home, collect information on taxes, utilities, warranties, and maintenance.

# Chapter 18

# Selecting an Agent

In this chapter
- ➤ Deciding whether to use an agent
- ➤ Selecting an agent
- ➤ Understanding listing agreements

Remember what you went through when you purchased a home? When you sell it, you have to go through it all again, but on the other side of the equation. Selling a home involves more than placing an ad and then fielding calls. You have to set the price, market the house, qualify buyers, and more. To help you handle all the details of selling, you can hire an agent. This chapter helps you decide whether to use an agent or not, then explains how to select a good one.

If you decide to sell the home yourself, see Chapter 22, which covers FSBOs (for-sale-by-owners).

## Should You Use an Agent or Sell Alone?

Why go without an agent? To save money. Many sellers don't want to pay the commission on selling a home. On a $100,000 home, you can save about $6,000 if you sell it yourself.

But that money is hard earned, and you have to be prepared mentally and psychologically. Selling a home yourself involves a lot of work and time. Before you proceed, consider what an agent can do for you. Then consider what it takes to sell your home yourself. After reviewing this information, you should be able to make your decision.

# What an Agent Can Do for You

As you know from buying a home, there are a lot of i's to dot and t's to cross in the process. An agent has experience as a salesperson and as a real estate expert to help you through this. Here are some of the things an agent can do for you:

*Help you set the listing price.* You'll want the most money you can get from your home, but a home that's priced too high will just sit there. And you won't like it one little bit. A good price is the first step for a successful sale. An agent can help determine the ideal asking price by looking at comparable homes in the area. If the house down the street sold for $115,000 and is nearly identical to yours, you should be able to get at least $115,000. The agent can help you collect the sales data to back up your sales price.

*Make suggestions on repairs and renovations.* An agent knows what buyers look for when they tour a home. Does a deck really add value? Or do most buyers ignore it? An agent can turn an objective eye on your home and tell you what problems stick out and what changes you should consider making.

*Screen potential buyers.* Do you want to open your home to every Curious Carole and Nosey Ned? Or do you want to spend that time showing the home to buyers who are really interested? An agent can help screen buyers. Are the buyers serious? Is this home appropriate for them? Can they afford it? Or are they just sight-seeing, at your expense?

*Help qualify buyers.* You want to attract buyers who are really looking for a home, and you want buyers who can afford yours. Many home buyers don't know what they can afford. You shouldn't waste time showing your home to anyone who doesn't have two nickels to rub together. Instead, an agent can financially prequalify the buyers to make sure they can afford your home.

*Market the house.* An agent will add your home information to the multiple listing service (MLS), a computerized collection of all listed homes in your market. Other agents use this service to find matches to their buyers. For example, a couple may be looking for a home just like yours. If your home is listed and an agent searches the MLS for one like it, your listing will appear in her search. This service helps bring buyers to your home. In addition to the MLS, the agent will have other strategies for marketing your home — open houses, ads, flyers, and so on. Some of the more motivated buyers are people from out of town who have only a weekend to look for a home. These buyers usually work with an agent.

*Handle negotiations.* There's a lot of thrusting and parrying during a negotiation. A good agent can keep the deal alive. Often buyers feel uncomfortable dealing directly with a seller. They think they'll offend you when they offer considerably less than the list price. So rather than offer, they'll just walk away. An agent, on the other hand, is a mediator. Buyers have no qualms about telling an agent what's wrong with the house and how much they think the house is worth. Your agent has the resources to show the buyer the true market value of your home.

*Overseeing the closing process.* Once an offer is accepted, there's still more work to be done — paperwork that has to be completed, inspections that have to be responded to, and more. An agent can help you manage the final hurdles up to and including the closing.

> **Do It Yourself?**
>
> The best time to sell a home yourself is in a hot market, when homes in the area are selling quickly. The worst time to sell is in a slow market, when homes are not moving so well. Also, it's riskier to sell a home yourself when you have to move in a hurry, because selling it yourself can take longer.

## Going It Alone

If you consider what an agent can do and say, "I can do that," you may still want to sell your home yourself. Keep in mind that about 65% of for-sale-by-owner (FSBO) sales don't go through. The sellers eventually take the home off the market, or the seller tries for a while and then hires an agent. That doesn't mean you should give up. It just means you should be prepared for the difficulties and the delays of selling your home yourself.

To sell your own home successfully, it helps to have experience with sales. If you don't like the sales game, you won't enjoy selling your home. You should be familiar with the current real estate market, including details of other homes listed in your area. What's the asking price of these homes? What was the selling price of comparable homes in the area? You'll also need to know what's involved in buying a home. You should know about appraisals, inspections, sales contracts, and more. You'll need some up-front money for advertising and for hiring consultants. And you'll need a thick skin. People can make hurtful comments about your house. You can't let those comments affect you.

An agent sometimes helps a buyer arrange financing. Unless the buyer has an agent, you have to assume the role of financial expert. You have to qualify buyers yourself. Can the buyer actually afford your home? You may also have to educate the buyer about getting financing. The deal isn't done until the buyer has the loan, so you'll be motivated to help the buyer get one. Are you comfortable asking buyers how much they earn and how much they have in the bank?

You'll need time to prepare for the sale: to handle sales calls and show the house. With an agent, you don't have to worry about daytime showings. The agent will handle these for you. Without an agent, you have to be available seven days a week, 24 hours a day.

Selling your home also requires research. You have to prepare buyer's qualification forms and information sheets about your home. You have to advertise, answer sales calls, show the property, and more. You should know how many square feet your home is, how many rooms, when the furnace was installed, when the house was built, and more. You should be an expert about your home and your property.

Unless you're incredibly lucky, you won't sell your house the first day it goes on the market. It may take a while and, while you wait, you have to be patient. A buyer won't come to the house if you're frustrated and growl into the telephone when he calls.

In the meantime, you'll receive dozens of calls from agents who want to represent you. They'll circle around, waiting until you become so fed up with the frustrations of selling your home yourself that you'll leap at the chance to hire one of them.

# Using an Agent

Instead of choosing the first agent who offers to list your home, you should select the person with more care. This person will have a lot of responsibility; you want someone who's committed to making the sale and with whom you feel comfortable.

A good way to find an agent is to ask friends and neighbors. Who sold their house? How long was it on the market? Did they get the asking price? Did the sellers think they could get more or did they think they got a good deal? Most sellers will remember bad experiences vividly; by asking around, you'll find out whom to avoid and, with luck, you'll also identify the agent to use.

You can also check your local paper for advertisements or visit a local broker's office.

## Quizzing the Agent

Once you have a few agents in mind, you may want to talk to each one on the phone or set up a meeting. You can use the following checklist to interview the agent(s):

How long have you been a real estate agent? _____ years

What professional organizations do you belong to?

Do you belong to a franchise? ❑ Yes ❑ No

Do you work as an agent full time? ❑ Yes ❑ No

How many homes have you listed in the past six months? _____

How many homes have you sold in the past six months? _____

Do you have access to the multiple listing service? ❑ Yes ❑ No

Where do you advertise? _____

What is your commission? _____

References _____

_____

_____

_____

_____

_____

### Get the List

Ask for a few recent listings, call these sellers, and ask about their experience with the agent. Your agent should be happy to give you some names. If he isn't, consider using a different agent.

## Listing Presentation

A potential agent should also complete a detailed listing presentation. This presentation should include:

➤ Information about the agent.

➤ Information about the housing market, such as how many homes are for sale in your area.

➤ Information about your home. For example, the agent may make suggestions about repairs that you should make.

➤ What the agent will do to sell the home. For example, how she will advertise the home and what information she'll generate, such as flyers or information sheets.

➤ All recent comparable sales and pending sales in your area, including detailed listings of the home information — number of storeys, number of bedrooms, number of baths, other rooms, other amenities (fireplace, basement, special features), the list date, list price, sale date, and selling price of the homes.

The agent may also include the MLS listings and pictures of the comparable homes.

Using the information from this report, the agent should then recommend an asking price for your home. The agent may give a range. For example, she may give you a price for a 30-day sale, a 60-day sale, and a 90-day sale. The agent who suggests the highest price for your home is not necessarily the one you should choose. After all, you want to sell the place, not just admire the fancy price tag.

## Signing a Listing Contract

Once you agree to use an agent, she'll ask you to sign a listing contract, which gives her the right to list the home. This section teaches you about the different types of contracts and what a contract should include.

## Types of Contracts

The contract basically spells out who gets the commission. Here are the most common:

**Exclusive listing**  This gives the agent's company the right to sell your house for a specified period. Your agent will likely encourage you to sign this type of contract, because she'll get the commission no matter who sells the property. If your brother Joe buys the house, your agent still gets the commission. But the commission may be slightly lower.

**Multiple listing**  With a multiple listing, the agent has the exclusive right to sell your house, but will also list it on the Multiple Listing System, which is accessible to all the agents in the area who belong to the MLS network.

### Open Houses

Many agents recommend an open house to show off your home to as many people as possible. In fact, open houses seldom result in sales. Agents like them, though, because they enable them to meet lots of potential clients. If you think an open house will disrupt your life unnecessarily, don't have one.

## What the Contract Should Include

Your listing agreement should state the following:

*Length of the contract.* Contracts usually range from 90 to 180 days, and you can extend them if you want. Be sure you don't sign a contract that is automatically extended. Also, a shorter contract may be better; at the end of the period, you can reevaluate your situation. Why isn't the house selling? Do you need a different agent?

*How long the agent is protected after the agreement expires.* If an agent finds a buyer but the contract has expired, the agent will want the commission anyway. Usually, the agent is protected for 30 to 60 days after the expiration. That means he gets the commission if a buyer returns after he showed the buyer the house while the listing was in effect.

*The commission rate.* The commission is based on the sale price. Six percent is common, but the commission rate is negotiable.

### Give Me a Break

Your agent may give you a break on the commission if you use him to list your current home and find your next home. It can't hurt to ask.

*A statement of the condition of property.* Are you selling the property as is? Or are you making repairs? If so, what will be repaired? What will be changed?

*A marketing plan.* The agreement should spell out how the agent plans to market the house. Where will the home be advertised? Will the agent hold open houses? If so, how often? What else will be done? Will the agent create flyers? Signs? How soon will the home be entered in the MLS listing? Will the agent schedule a showing for other agents?

*A statement of the price and terms for the sale of the house.* For example, the agreement should include the list price, the amount of deposit you require, and the terms of the sale you'll accept. Also, the agreement should list what's included in the sale — appliances, draperies, and so on.

*Permissions.* The agreement should grant explicit permission for the agent to do certain things such as use a lockbox for your door key, put a sign in the yard, and so on.

## Getting Out of a Listing

If you're unhappy with an agent, you can't just fire him. You've signed an agreement. If you're not satisfied with the agent's performance, start by asking yourself what you're dissatisfied with. Are you unhappy because you haven't sold the house in the first month? Or are you unhappy because the house has been on the market for one month, but there's still no sign in the yard, and you haven't had a single showing?

You'll be anxious to sell, but you have to keep your expectations reasonable. If they aren't, you need to be more patient. If you have reasonable expectations that are unfulfilled, you should voice your concerns to the agent. Tell him what you expect to be done, then give him a second chance.

If you're still unsatisfied, ask for your listing back. The agent doesn't have to give the listing back, but he may. If he doesn't, you may want to complain to the agent's broker, to the real estate board, and to the Better Business Bureau. If you become a nuisance, the agent may change his mind.

You also can't just take the house off the market for any reason. If you have a legitimate reason (for example, a death in the family), the agent will most likely be understanding. If you don't have a legitimate reason (for example, you want to take the house off the market because you found a buyer yourself), the agent isn't likely to be so accommodating. In fact, if you proceed with the sale, you'll still have to pay a commission to the agent. That's what you agreed to do, and that's what you're — legally and morally — obligated to do.

It's best to ask the agent up front about the circumstances under which you can take the house off the market.

# The Least You Need to Know

Preparing for the sale of your home requires a lot of work and a lot of knowledge about sales and the real estate market. To help you with this task, you may want to hire an agent. An agent not only knows about sales, she should have experience in the housing market.

➤ You should first decide whether you want to use an agent or not. An agent can help you set your listing price, suggest repairs, screen buyers, market the house, and negotiate the deal.

➤ Many sellers decide to sell their homes themselves to save the 6% commission to the agent. If you decide to sell your home yourself, you should have experience with sales, know about your house and the current market, have an understanding of financing a home, and have the time and patience to do the work and deal with potential buyers.

➤ You should ask for recommendations from friends and family when searching for an agent. Ask about an agent's background, experience, number of listings, number of homes sold, education, and more.

➤ The agent you select should prepare a marketing report for your home that includes information about comparable homes in your area (features of the home, listing price, sales price, date listed, and date sold). In addition, this report should include a recommendation on a list price for your home and a description of what the agent will do to market your home.

➤ Your agent will require you to sign a listing agreement that gives him permission to list and sell your home. This agreement should include the duration of the contract, the commission, the marketing plan for the home, the listing price of your home, a description of the terms you'll accept, and other information.

# Chapter 19

# Pricing and Marketing the House

---

**In this chapter**

➤ Setting the listing price

➤ Deciding on the terms

➤ Figuring your net profit or loss

➤ Getting the attention of buyers

➤ Showing the buyer your home

---

Every year, more than 200,000 houses go on the market. How many will sell? And how fast will they sell? The answers to these questions depend on a lot of factors, the most important being the price. This chapter first covers how to set the listing price for your home, then covers the marketing techniques for getting buyers to your house.

## Setting the Listing Price

It's easy to make a mistake when considering the price to ask for your house. As a seller, you want to get the highest possible price, but you also want to avoid the many pitfalls.

*Pitfall 1* Pricing the house as high as you can and worrying about lowering the price later. Mistake! When an agent and potential buyers see your overpriced house, they'll most likely move on. By the time you wise up and set a more reasonable price, your house will have been on the market for a while. In this case, the property just sits, and the price is lowered and lowered and lowered until it finally sells. As the price falls, buyers may think there's something wrong with the house, since it has been on the market for so long.

*Pitfall 2* Coming up with a reasonable price and setting the listing price there. Again, mistake. Most buyers expect to pay less than the asking price, except in very hot markets. You should leave room for negotiating.

In an active market, a reasonable asking price, near or at the selling price of similar homes, should attract many buyers. You'll be in a stronger negotiating position to hold to your price.

*Pitfall 3* Determining the profit you need and setting the price accordingly. Another mistake. Of course, you should consider what you hope to gain from the sale. This enables you to plan for the next home you purchase. But you can get for your house only what someone is willing to pay. What you need and what you expect should not really factor into pricing your home.

Setting the price is a tricky balancing act. This chapter will give you some advice on setting the right price.

## Studying Comparables

The best way to find out what a home like yours is worth is to look at the selling price of similar homes in your area. It's critical to compare similar homes. The first determining factor is the area. Don't compare a home in one neighborhood to a similar house in a neighborhood across town. Remember: location, location, location.

The second determining factor is the home's attributes — how many bedrooms, how many baths, number of other rooms (dining room, living room, family room), amenities (fireplace, hardwood floors, and so on). You may find some houses similar to yours and some that are comparable.

Your agent's marketing report should contain a survey of both types of home that have recently sold or are on the market.

Once you know the selling price of similar and comparable homes, you can compare your house and come up with a reasonable price. For instance, if one house has a little more to offer than your house, you should price your house a little lower. Others will have less to offer and you can price your house a little higher. This method helps you to price your home based on market data — what people are willing to pay.

Looking at the listing prices for houses that are currently on the market can help, but keep in mind that these homes haven't sold. The owners might be dreaming. And the selling price could be significantly lower than the listing price.

**Cold or Hot Spread?**

Figure out the percentage by which the listing price differs from the selling price to measure the temperature of the market. For instance, if houses are selling for 95% of the list price, the market is hot; 80 to 90%, the market is weak. The difference, or spread, may vary depending on area.

## Getting an Appraisal

If you can't come up with a listing price by looking at comparable homes, get an appraiser to help in setting the price. You can hire an independent appraiser for around $250 to $300 to provide you with a professional opinion on the market value of the home. The appraiser will study similar homes, look at yours, and come up with an evaluation. You may need an appraisal especially if you and your agent can't agree on the value of the home.

Getting the appraisal beforehand can help in another way. When a buyer applies for a loan, the lender will require an independent appraisal. If your home is appraised for more than the asking price, the lender will likely approve the loan. If your home is appraised for less, the lender may not give the buyer the loan he needs to pay for the home, and you may have to renegotiate the offer. It helps to find out what the house is worth before you start taking offers.

The lender will still order an independent appraisal. But if your appraiser is trustworthy, the two appraisals should be within range of each other.

## How the Market Affects Price

In a hot market, houses are in demand. There are more buyers than sellers, by a ratio as high as 8 to 1. This means that a buyer may overlook a few maintenance items, you may get top price for your house, and your house may sell more quickly.

In a medium market, there are a lot of buyers and a lot of sellers. In this market, you can expect to wait one to three months to sell your home, and the price and terms will require some compromise on both sides. Because there are a lot of houses on the market, a buyer may base his decision about a purchase on the condition of the home. For example, if the buyer sees two similar homes, one in good condition and the other needing work, the buyer will likely select the one in good condition.

In a cool market, there are a lot of sellers, but few buyers. You'll have to add incentives to entice a buyer out of hiding.

## Deciding What Else to Offer

In addition to determining the listing price, consider what else you want to offer the buyer. In a hot market, you may not have to offer incentives. In a slow market, you may have to entice buyers with something extra.

For example, you may agree to pay for some repairs or offer a redecorating allowance. You might offer $1,000 for new carpeting. One seller offered to throw in his car with the deal.

If you find a prospective buyer, but the buyer can't get financing, you may help with financing. For example, you may buy down the mortgage rate or take back a mortgage. Creative financing such as this is covered in Chapter 12. Chapter 20 also covers some strategies for financing.

You may purchase a home warranty (around $300 a year) that protects the major systems and appliances in the house. This warranty may make an older home more attractive to the buyer.

You should have a good idea of what you want to offer the buyer so that you're prepared for the costs involved in selling.

## Figuring Your Net Proceeds

When you sell your home, you'll most likely be buying another one. So you need to determine what you can afford to pay for your new home. This may depend on the proceeds from the sale of your existing home.

For this reason, you should consider several scenarios to determine your net profit (or loss).

*Consider different selling prices.* Doing so may help you come up with the lowest amount you can accept. Consider any repairs you must make. If you need a new roof, be sure to account for the expense. Know beforehand what other incentives you want to offer the seller. For example, if you plan to offer financial incentives, be sure to include these costs in your estimate of your net proceeds.

*Know the closing costs you'll incur.* Some closing costs are traditionally paid for by the seller. For example, the buyer may require a survey of your property, which you will have to provide.

### Any Penalties?

In deciding to sell your home, check your mortgage agreement to see if you'll have to pay a penalty for repaying the mortgage when you complete the sale. Sometimes a buyer can assume your mortgage; sometimes you can take the mortgage with you if you buy another home; but sometimes you'll have to pay a penalty equivalent to three months of interest on the mortgage or more. In extreme cases, the lender can refuse to let you repay the mortgage at all.

Taking at look at the financial aspect of the sale will help you evaluate the offers you receive. It gives you a game plan for negotiating.

# Getting the Attention of Buyers

Your agent should provide you with a complete plan for marketing the house and attracting buyers. There are many strategies for doing so. The most obvious is the listing in the MLS database, which provides key information about your home, including the size of the rooms, age of the house, and so on, to agents throughout the city or town where your home is located.

In addition to the MLS entry, your agent may also create an information sheet to distribute to potential buyers. This information sheet may include a photo of the home, the address, and the listing price. In addition, the agent may write some inviting copy for the information

### Your Home, Your Idea

Have a flair for writing copy? You may want to make suggestions to the agent. After all, no one knows your house and its best features better than you. Feel free to tell the agent what you think are its best selling points.

sheet, such as "Great curb appeal!" Or "Beautiful mature trees. Great yard for dogs, kids, and cookouts!" The information will stress the most positive aspects of your house.

The agent may also schedule open houses (see the section "Holding an Open House," later in this chapter). For an open house, the agent will most likely put an advertisement in the paper and put up signs around the neighborhood.

The agent may use other means to advertise your house. For example, in some areas, a televised real estate show on Saturday or Sunday mornings carries listings of homes on the market. Maybe your agent will showcase your home on the show. Your agent may also include a listing of your home in the neighborhood flyers and brochures that circulate frequently in grocery stores and other locations.

The agent may also use an extensive network of other agents, buyers, and associates to add good word-of-mouth exposure for your home.

The types of advertising the agent does should be agreed upon when you sign the listing contract.

# Showing Your Home

As part of the agent's services, he will arrange for showings. Other agents may also pull your listing from the MLS and arrange for a showing through your agent. This section covers the preparation for the showing.

## Scheduling a Showing

If you had to run home and unlock the house each time someone wanted to show it, you'd quickly exhaust yourself. Usually the agent arranges to make the home accessible to other agents. For instance, the agent may put a lockbox on your front door with the keys inside. If another agent wants to visit the home, he calls your agent, who calls back to verify that the agent is really an agent and not some thief looking for a quick way into the house. Then your agent will tell the other agent the combination to the lock so that he can show the house.

If you don't use a lockbox, the agent might keep the key available at his office, where other agents can pick it up. Only agents can show the house.

You should count on showings occurring at the most inconvenient times: just when you sit down to dinner or when you climb into the bath. After all, most people are free to look at homes just when you're free to start enjoying yourself.

You can always say no, but what if that particular person is the most likely buyer?

You can also stay in the house during the showing, but your presence may make the buyer uncomfortable, and you want the buyer to feel as comfortable as possible. For this reason, you'll probably spend a lot of time driving aimlessly around your neighborhood or sitting at some fast food restaurant for an hour or so.

If you're like my husband and me, you may spy a little on the buyers. You'll try to catch a glimpse of them as they come to the house or time them as they tour the house by driving by and seeing whether their car is still there. The longer they stay, the more hopeful you'll get.

If you have a dog, you may have to arrange to lock him up during the day for showings or take him with you during showings in the evenings.

# Getting the House Ready

When you get the call for a showing, you need to get the house ready as quickly as possible. This is another hassle of having your home on the market; you have to keep it clean and tidy all the time.

You should have done your major cleaning before the house went on the market (see Chapter 17). You now need to do just a quick tidying for a showing. Put away any clutter. Pick up the newspapers. Put dirty dishes in the dishwasher.

Also, try to set the mood for the showing. For example, if it's winter, light a fire in the fireplace. Simmer some potpourri on the stove so the

## Time to Lower the Price

When you've had a lot of showings and no particularly bad comments, consider reducing the price. This may be the reason you haven't received any offers.

home smells nice. If the showing is during the day, open the windows and let sunshine in. Turn on all the lights. You want the house to look bright and cheerful, not drab and dreary. Finally, put on some soft music.

## Dealing with Criticism

After potential buyers take a look through your house, their agent will most likely ask them what they thought of the place. Their agent will then call your agent and relay the news. "Loved the fireplace. Hated the small bathroom."

Be prepared for criticism. It might hurt, especially after you went to so much trouble, but you want to see the house through the buyers' eyes. If three buyers say the carpeting in the living room is pathetic, you can do something about it.

Buyers will critique the house and nit-pick over details. You probably do too when you look at a house for sale. Don't take offense.

## Holding an Open House

In addition to showings, your agent may schedule open houses, usually on a Saturday or Sunday. You can think of an open house as one long showing with more browsers than buyers.

If you think an open house is a surefire way to sell your house and you'll have rooms and rooms full of buyers, think again. A survey of U.S. realtors found that just 3% of home owners found their homes through an open house. Sometimes an agent finds a buyer through an open house, but more often the agent finds new clients through an open house. Does that mean that you shouldn't have open houses? Not necessarily.

Even if they attract mostly lookers, open houses call attention to your home. The agent will advertise the open house in the paper and will put up signs. If a potential buyer is looking through the paper or driving by, he may notice your home, even if he doesn't stop.

**Not Too Many**

Be sure not to schedule too many open houses. Consider how you'd react if you saw the same house advertised over and over again in the newspaper. You don't want potential buyers to think your house is a loser by overexposing it.

Also, even the lookers can help. Maybe they aren't in the market for a house, but they may know of someone who is. Word of mouth can't hurt.

But don't feel obligated to hold an open house. It's still your decision.

# The Least You Need to Know

How quickly you sell your home often depends on the listing price you set and how well you advertise it. Your agent can help you come up with a reasonable listing price and will help you get buyers to your home.

➤ The best way to figure your listing price is to study data on comparable sales in your area. Check the listing price and selling price of these homes. Also, see when they were listed and when they were sold to find out how long they were on the market.

➤ After you decide on your listing price, think about the terms you want to offer to the buyer. You should have a good idea of what you'll pay on the buyer's behalf as well as what you'll be required to pay at closing.

➤ When you know the price and terms, you can come up with different scenarios that would work for you. Having a target bottom line will help you evaluate any offers you receive.

➤ Your agent will most likely market the house by adding your home's description to the multiple listing service, by creating advertisements and flyers, by arranging for showings, and by holding open houses.

**Home is the place where,
When you go there,
They have to take you in.**

**—Robert Frost**

# Chapter 20

# Negotiating Offers

## In this chapter

➤ Dealing with other agents

➤ Evaluating an offer

➤ Making a counteroffer

➤ Accepting an offer

➤ What to do if you don't get any offers

➤ Helping the buyer with financing

Consider all the cleaning, repairing, decision making, marketing, and worrying you've done with the explicit goal of getting an offer on your home. All that work for one simple piece of paper that says, "Yes! I want to buy your home." What should you expect when you receive an offer? How can you decide whether you should accept an offer? What happens if you don't get any offers? This chapter covers these questions and more.

## Dealing with Other Agents

When you sign an agreement with an agent, the agent agrees to do her best to sell your home at the price you decided on. The agent is

**Buyer's Agents**

In some parts of the country, buyers can hire their own agent, called a buyer's agent. In this relationship, the agent represents the buyer exclusively and is not obliged to disclose information to the seller if it will not further the cause of her client.

entirely responsible to you and has only your interest in mind. Getting the best price is in the agent's best interest. The higher the price, the more the agent stands to earn on commission.

The buyers will likely have an agent as well. Sometimes the agent, in fact, works for you, because you pay his commission out of the selling price. In some cases, he represents the buyer, not you. It's important to know the difference.

Although the agent is helping the buyers, he is in most cases being paid by you. Therefore, he owes his loyalty to you. He should pass along all information regarding offers. If a buyer offers $100,000 but tells the agent he'll go to $105,000, the agent should let you know.

This means that when an agent presents an offer you should ask him if he represents you or the buyer. Depending on the type of agent, you can expect to receive different information from the agent.

# Evaluating an Offer

Before you even think about evaluating an offer, you should spend some time thinking about what you want from the sale of your home. You should have in mind several possible prices and sets of terms, as described in Chapter 19. What is the lowest price you'll accept? Which terms are okay? Which terms are not okay? You should discuss the price and terms with your agent.

Knowing your bottom line can help you and your agent evaluate offers. You can compare the offers to your objectives to see how they match up.

When potential buyers want to make an offer, they'll sit down with their agent and draw up an offer of purchase and sale. The buyer's agent will contact your agent and convey the offer, usually in person. The buyer's agent will then give your agent the document. You should accept only written offers.

The buyers will give you a period of one or two days to respond to the offer. During that time, you and your agent can evaluate the offer, as described next.

## What an Offer Should Include

You can expect an offer to include the following:

➤ The address and legal description of the property (lot, block, and square recorded in government records).

➤ The names of the brokers involved.

➤ The price, down payment, loan amount, and the amount of the deposit.

➤ A time limit for the response to the offer, getting financing, and closing on the house.

➤ Conditions that must be met.

➤ Other provisions, such as personal property that's included; how adjustments, damages, and other special circumstances are handled; and so on.

## What Price and at What Terms?

The first thing you want to know is "How much?" How much did the buyer offer? Unless you're in a really hot market, the buyer will most likely offer less than your listing price. Before you tear up the offer, though, look at how much less. Is the price close enough? Also, look at the terms of the contract. If the buyer offered less, did she give more on the terms?

Next, look at the money you have in hand — the deposit. How much did the buyer put down? Is it sufficient? Does the deposit show that the buyer is serious about purchasing the home?

Also, ask your agent if the buyer is well qualified.

## Checking the Contingencies

Look through any conditions the buyer has included in the contract. For instance, the buyer may make the purchase conditional on financing.

As you look through the conditions, ask yourself whether they're

**Let Me Stay, Please**

If you can't move out by the date specified, and the buyer isn't in a hurry to move in, you may negotiate a short-term rental agreement. You sell the house to the buyer then rent it back for a few months until you can move out.

acceptable. Are they reasonable? For example, a financing condition is pretty common and pretty reasonable, but you don't have to accept it.

Look also at the limits of the condition and note how they're removed. For instance, the buyer needs financing, but if he doesn't specify how much time he can take to get it, the condition may not be acceptable.

You should also determine whether the buyers are likely to qualify for a loan. Their agent or yours can tell you. You should know when the buyers obtain financing, and you should know what happens if they don't get financing.

Some buyers make their purchase conditional on a satisfactory inspection. If you did your job in preparing the home, you should know where the problems lie. Either give the buyer a period in which to have the house inspected and ask for a copy of the report, or strike the condition from the offer.

The sale may also be conditional on the buyers selling their home. This should give you serious pause. Do you really want to tie up your sale with the sale of an unknown home? If you agree to this contingency, you should ask your agent to evaluate the buyer's current home at the price listed. Is it listed now? Is it priced reasonably? Is it in good condition? Is it likely to sell? You may want to include some protection for yourself in case their home doesn't sell. For example, you may keep your home on the market and give the buyers right of first refusal. If you get another offer during that time, the first buyers can remove the contingency and buy the house, or they can withdraw their offer.

## Checking the Time Limits

The contract should specify certain time limits. For example, you'll want the buyers to apply for a mortgage and have the home inspected within a certain period.

In addition, the buyers will want you to respond to the offer by a certain time and to move out of the home by a certain time. The buyers will likely specify a closing date. Be sure this date is acceptable.

# Making a Counteroffer

After evaluating an offer, you have three options. You can say, "Yes! We'll take it." In this case, see the next section, "Accepting an Offer."

You can say, "No! Forget it," roll the offer into a little ball, and hurl it at the cat. That's the end of the process.

Your third option is to make a counteroffer. You may raise the price or change the terms. You may make the changes directly on the original offer or submit a new one.

Be sure to spell out all the changes you want to make. The buyer will assume you found everything else acceptable. If you're unsure, write in your conditions again.

Your agent will relay any counteroffers back to the buyers' agent, who will relay the offer to the buyers. The buyers can accept the offer or can counter again.

# Accepting an Offer

Your offer is accepted when both parties sign the same agreement; that is, when you accept the buyers' original offer or a counteroffer made by them, or when the buyers accept your counteroffer.

Congratulations! You've sold your home. You should get a copy of the accepted offer and prepare for the final step — the closing. This topic is discussed in Chapter 21.

# What to Do if You Don't Get Any Offers

You're sitting in your house patiently waiting and waiting and waiting. What if you don't get any nibbles? What if your house has been on the market, but not one person has made an offer? When you aren't getting any offers, you should evaluate the situation to find out where the problem lies.

*Have you given yourself enough time?* If you don't have an offer in the first week, it's not time to give up. Selling a home can take several months or more, depending on the current market. You should ask yourself whether you're being overly anxious or whether there's another problem.

*Has the house received enough exposure?* Are people coming to see it? Have you had a lot of showings? How many? How many calls? How many open houses? *Were the open houses well attended?* A buyer can't buy the house unless he knows it's for sale. If buyers haven't been looking, you can't expect them to buy. If this is the problem, discuss with your agent other options. Has the agent done enough advertising? Held enough open houses?

*What's the current market like?* Is it hot, warm, lukewarm, cool, cold, frosty? Real estate professionals like to use a lot of hot/cold and hard/soft terms to describe the market. For a seller, hot is good, cold is bad. Many things can determine the current market. For example, what's the current level of interest rates? If rates are sky high, buyers may be unable to afford a home. If you're selling in a cool or cold market, you may want to wait for better conditions. If you can't wait, you may want to offer additional incentives for the buyer, such as help with financing.

*What is your neighborhood like?* Remember, location is the most important factor in determining the desirability of a home. If you live in a war zone, you may have a hard time selling your house. There's not much you can do about a bad neighborhood. You can try to improve it, which is most likely not going to happen overnight. Or you can lower the price.

*What's the condition of the house?* Go back to Chapter 17 and look through your assessment of the condition of the house. Does the home have curb appeal? What problems do you see? Ask the opinions of others. For instance, you should get feedback from the showings. Why weren't the buyers interested? You may also want to get a professional opinion from an inspector. If the home's condition is the problem, you may want to make improvements or lower the price.

*Is the price too high?* If you've had a few nibbles, what price was offered? If you're getting offers, but at a much lower price, you may need to reduce the asking price. Also, get feedback from your showings. What did potential buyers say about the price? What does your agent think about the price? If you're having serious concerns about the price, you should have an appraisal done.

**Close Sometimes Counts**

If you're close on the deal, you may not want to push it. Consider taking the deal and being satisfied. Any time you make a counteroffer, you give the potential buyer the opportunity to walk away. The better the offer, the more you risk losing it when you make a counteroffer.

*What terms are you offering (or not offering)?* Are you offering reasonable terms? Do you need to add incentives to help the buyer? Is there a particular problem with this property that needs to be addressed?

# Should You Help with Financing?

When your house won't sell, many sellers consider helping with financing. You may decide to help the buyer in a number of ways. You may buy down the mortgage or take back a second mortgage (basically, you lend the buyers the money). Alternative financing is covered in Chapter 12.

## Multiple Offers

In a hot market, you may receive more than one offer at the same time, especially if you live in a popular neighborhood. When you receive multiple offers, your agent can help you to evaluate them. The highest price doesn't always indicate the best offer, although it's pretty persuasive.

Before you agree to help with financing, consider the buyers' motivation. Why can't the buyers get a conventional loan? Do they have bad credit? Will their income cover their debt? Don't they have the money for a down payment? There are usually good reasons why a lender won't lend to a buyer. Are you willing to do what a more experienced lender won't do?

If interest rates are really high, a buyer may have more difficulty than usual qualifying for a loan. Or perhaps you want to sell to a couple that just graduated from college. They have good income potential, but just don't have any money for a down payment now. As an individual, you don't have to conform to the same strict guidelines as an institutional lender.

If you decide to help the buyer, you need to take several precautions. Lending money is risky. You should first check out the buyer. Do a thorough credit report. (See Chapter 12 for information on obtaining a credit check.) Get an explanation of any problems. If the buyers have a history of missed payments, are you sure you want to count on them to pay you back, even if they do look like really nice people?

Make sure the buyers are committed to the property. For example, if you take back a mortgage on the home for the buyers, you might insist on a big down payment. It's also a good idea to lend over a short term. Make sure you're not giving your money away. Insist on a fair interest rate.

Be sure to arrange a formal legal agreement. In the agreement, spell out the terms. When do you expect to be paid back? What is the penalty for late payments? Have your lawyer review the agreement.

Finally, consider the worst-case scenario. What if the buyers skip town to Tupelo, Mississippi, with four months' worth of overdue payments? Can you get your missing payments? How do you foreclose on a property? What's the cost of foreclosure?

# The Least You Need to Know

When you receive an offer, you should first review it to decide whether you find it acceptable. If it's not, you should plan a strategy for getting an acceptable offer; for example, countering with another offer to the buyers. Once you have a signed offer, you've sold your house!

➤ Your agent represents your interests. The buyer will also most likely be working with an agent. If the buyer uses a buyer's agent, the agent represents only the interests of the buyer. If the buyer doesn't have a buyer's agreement with the agent, the agent actually works for you and should pass along any and all information about the price and terms the buyer is willing to accept.

➤ Look over any conditions included in the contract. Make sure that they're reasonable, acceptable, and limited.

➤ You don't have to accept a buyer's first offer. You may want to counter with your own offer. Countering continues until one party walks away or until the deal is signed by both parties. Be careful not to haggle over frivolous terms.

➤ If you aren't getting any offers on your home, determine whether you've allowed enough time and whether the house has had enough exposure. Take a look at the market conditions, the condition of your home, the price, and terms to see whether you can pinpoint the problem.

➤ In a tough market, you might offer the buyer help with financing. Be careful! Vendor financing is risky. Be sure to get a thorough credit check on the buyers, and have your lawyer review or draft an agreement. Charge the going market rate for interest and try to keep the term of the loan short. Know the consequences of the worst-case scenario.

# Handling the Closing: Seller's Point of View

After months and months of waiting to sell your home, you may get an acceptable offer and then want to know, "Where's my money?" Money is handled at the closing. At this time, you hand over the deed and keys to your property, and the buyer hands over a cheque.

This usually occurs months after the offer, and requires some preparation time for you and the buyer. This chapter explains how to get ready for closing, what happens at closing, and what happens after closing.

# What Is Closing?

The term *closing* refers to the final step in the process of selling or buying a home. At this point, documents are signed, and money is exchanged.

The closing may be held at a lawyer's office or lending institution, depending on local custom.

The closing is scheduled after the buyers obtain financing and have met all other obligations. Your lawyer should let you know the precise time and place for the closing. The next section explains what has to happen before you can close on your house.

# What the Buyer Has to Do

Most of the preclosing work falls to the buyer. The buyer usually has to obtain financing, get insurance, and meet any other requirements of the lender. The buyer will also schedule a home inspection sometime before closing.

If the buyer encounters problems, you should know about them as soon as possible, especially problems that can jeopardize the deal. You and your agent should keep yourselves informed about the buyer's progress.

# What You Have to Do

In addition to checking up on the buyer, you have some responsibilities to meet. This section explains what you're expected to do.

## Termites and Other Critters

In some locations, you may need a termite inspection of the house. A termite inspection is sometimes the responsibility of the seller. Lenders won't approve a loan until the inspection is done, so you'll need to schedule the inspection. At the closing, you should bring the inspection report. If you have termites, you will have to have them treated. (I don't know why they use the term treated. It sounds as if the termites are checking into the Betty Ford Clinic. A more descriptive term would be terminated, zapped, poisoned, fried, whatever.)

## Collecting Documents

At the closing, you should expect to bring a copy of the sales contract, with documentation showing that contingencies have been removed and conditions have been met. For example, it a termite inspection is required, you have to show the original inspection report.

Bring receipts of paid utilities and taxes. You may have to show documentation of paid utilities.

Also, bring any information on your current loan. You should know the mortgage balance and the date to which you've paid, as well as any penalties you might incur as a result of paying off the mortgage before it's due. The money you receive from the buyers won't go directly to your pocket. You'll likely have to pay off the loan on your home. Your lawyer will arrange payoff at the date of closing.

## Hiring an Orchestrator

What if you closed on the house, but forgot to pay off your existing loan? What if you sold the house, but the deed wasn't transferred to the buyer's name? What if the buyers assumed the mortgage, but no one made a record of the transaction? You'd be in hot soup, that's what. To make sure everything is done, in the proper order, you need a lawyer to orchestrate the deal.

Your lawyer will handle the title to the property, collect the buyers' money, and conclude the sale. Your agent can recommend a lawyer or you can select a lawyer yourself.

The lawyer starts by collecting the sales agreement. This agreement is the blueprint for the proceedings. The lawyer will use the agreement to prepare a list of instructions for you, basically assigning you your homework.

At the closing, the lawyer collects all the necessary documents and prepares the documents for signatures. If you have to sign a million pieces of paper, glare at the lawyer. He's the paper-pusher in the deal.

The lawyer is also the money handler. He will calculate all figures and tell you who pays what — the total deposit amount, the down payment, the closing costs.

The lawyer will collect the money due from the sale and then hold

### Proration

A *proration* is an adjustment of a bill or payment paid in advance which allows you to recover some or all of the money. Suppose you pay your taxes in advance. In the six-month tax period when you sell your home, you'll live in the place for only three of those months. You should have to pay for those months, but not the others. To determine how much you have to pay and you much you get back from the buyer, your lawyer takes the total payment, divides it by 6 (the number of months) and then multiplies it by the number of months you're responsible for (3). Utility bills are often prorated, as well.

the money in trust, until the sale is final (usually when the deed is recorded, which is also done by the lawyer).

Finally, the lawyer will disburse (a fancy word for hand out) the money. The lawyer should take care of paying off your current loan and then pay you your remaining equity.

# Handling Problems

Most problems will crop up before closing and will have to be dealt with before you can close. Here are some common hurdles:

*Holdups in the loan process.* If the lender doesn't approve the loan, the buyer can't buy the house. For this reason, you'll want progress reports on the loan application. If a problem occurs, you should know how serious it is. Is the process just delayed? Is the process held up by something you must do? Or have the buyers been denied?

*Problems with the appraisal.* Before approving the loan, the lender will require an independent appraisal. A lender will approve a loan for as much as 95% of the appraised value or purchase price of a home, whichever is less. If the lender's appraisal comes in a lot lower than the selling price, your buyer may have problems. Either the buyer will have to come up with more money or the deal will fall through, especially if the buyer made the sale conditional on financing.

*Problems with the inspection.* If the inspection report turns up problems, and if the buyers had a condition in the contract for a successful inspection, they may ask you to make certain repairs or renegotiate the price. Your agent can help you deal with these problems. You can refuse to make the repairs and kill the deal, but you should realize that you'll likely be asked to make the same repairs on the next offer.

*Repairs required for loan approval.* Even if the buyers say it's okay to skip some repairs, the lender may require certain repairs.

*Problems with the title.* If the title search turns up problems, you have to clear them up before the closing. You can pay off a lien if you have a bad debt, or you can get the person with the claim to sign a release. If the claim is in error, you must have it corrected.

The details of the agreement are spelled out in the contract, so you shouldn't hear any surprises at closing. If you do, you can refer to the agreement. If disputes pop up, they usually pertain to the deposit, condition of property, or definition of personal property. Check the contract. If you can't come to an agreement, you may resort to mediation. A third party hears both sides and then makes a ruling. Some contracts will spell out how disputes are to be handled.

# What Happens at Closing?

At the closing, the buyers sign their loan agreements, and you sign over the deed. You also go over the final reckoning of closing costs. The closing costs you're expected to pay will vary depending on the local custom, the lender, and what you've agreed to in the sales agreement.

## Check the Numbers

You should get the figures and check them before closing. Your agent is experienced with the closing details, but you should check over the figures to ensure they're correct.

## Fees You Can Expect

Here are some of the fees you as seller may be expected to pay:

**Commission** You're responsible for the commission fee charged by your agent. This fee should be agreed upon as part of the listing agreement. Six percent of the selling price is common.

**Don't Sign**

If you note any discrepancies, don't sign the document. Signing means that you agree with the document. It's difficult to get agreements changed after you sign.

**Lawyer** If you've hired a lawyer, you'll be responsible for the lawyer's fees.

**Taxes** You may owe money for tax proration.

**Utilities** You have to pay your utility bills up to the date of closing.

## Sign on the Dotted Line

You'll be required to sign several documents at the closing. Before you sign, make sure the information is correct.

You'll also sign the deed transferring property to the buyer and a vendor affidavit. Then you turn over all your house keys, mailbox keys, and garage door openers to the buyer. After the deed is delivered, you'll receive the cheque for your proceeds.

# Moving Out!

When it's time to move out, you may have mixed emotions. You've sold your house, possibly made a profit, and may be moving on to another home. This makes you happy. On the other hand, you may really have enjoyed your old home and may have many good memories wrapped up in it. Just keep in mind that you'll make new memories in your new home.

Use the opportunity when packing to get rid of items you no longer need. Don't take everything with you. You may want to have a garage sale or donate items to charity. Packing or unpacking is also a good time to make an inventory of your possessions.

Contact the utility companies. Ask for a final reading so that you know what you owe. Also, have the buyer transfer utilities to her name. Buyers sometimes must make a cash deposit.

Fill out change of address cards.

Welcome the new buyers. The sellers of our first home left a bottle of wine with a nice note in the refrigerator. This was a pleasant surprise and made my husband and me really feel welcome in the house.

Start a house file. In this file, keep all the documents pertaining to the sale of your home. You will need this information when you file your tax returns.

# The Least You Need to Know

Closing is the final process in selling your home. At the closing, you sign documents and exchange money. A lot has to go on before you can close. After the closing, you receive your money and move on.

➤ Buyers have certain responsibilities to meet before closing, including securing a loan, getting insurance, and having the home inspected. You also have certain things to arrange: deed, utility bills, loan payoff.

➤ If there are problems with the loan, the appraisal, the title, or the inspection, they must be handled before the closing.

**Never ask of money
Where the spender thinks it went
Nobody was ever meant
To remember or invent
What he did with every cent.**

—**Robert Frost**

# Chapter 22

# Selling Your Home Yourself

## In this chapter

➤ Mapping out your strategy

➤ Pricing your home

➤ Marketing your home

➤ Showing your home

➤ Understanding financing

➤ Negotiating with the buyers

➤ Closing on the home

➤ Knowing when to call it quits

Approximately one in six home sales close without the work of an agent. Are you one of the six that can sell practically anything? Do you know a lot about your home and neighborhood? Do you understand the real estate market — financing, negotiating, and closing? If so, you may want to forego hiring an agent and sell your home yourself. Why go it alone? To save money. Agents typically charge a 6% commission. On a $100,000 house, that comes to $6,000!

Selling a home by yourself isn't easy. Chapter 18 discusses what you should expect if you want to go it alone and explains the services an agent can provide. If you've still made your way to this chapter, you're ready to get to work selling your home.

# Mapping Out Your Strategy

To begin with, you should understand the entire process of selling a home; then you can identify your strengths and weaknesses and see where you need help.

## Step 1: Get the Home Ready

This process is described in Chapter 17. You first inspect your home and then determine the repairs and improvements you need to make. If you're having trouble deciding what to do, you may hire a professional inspector. You may also hire contractors to do some of the repair work, if any is needed.

## Step 2: Set the Listing Price

Pricing your home yourself is covered later in this chapter in the section "Setting the Price." You may also want to consult agents or home appraisers in setting your price.

## Step 3: Market the Home

Before a buyer can be interested in your home, she'll have to know it's for sale. The section "Marketing Your Home," later in this chapter, covers how to advertise and show your home. If you have trouble getting the attention of buyers, you may want to consider listing your home with an agent.

## Step 4: Help the Buyer Get Financing

Getting an offer from a buyer is one thing; getting an offer from a buyer who can actually pay for the home is something entirely different. As part of the sales process, you should qualify the buyers so that you're sure they can obtain financing for the home. Consider visiting several lenders and collecting information from them on the lending process. Financing is covered later in this chapter.

## Step 5: Negotiate the Sale

Negotiating involves coming to an agreement with the buyers on price and terms. It also involves drawing up a binding contract that protects your interests. You should hire a real estate lawyer to help you with the contracts. Hiring a lawyer is covered later.

## Step 6: Close on the Home

Closing is the final process of signing papers, transferring ownership, and collecting money. To help you with the closing, you should use a lawyer.

# Using an Agent

Once you put that FOR SALE sign in your yard, be prepared for a cavalcade of real estate agents asking you to list your house with them. You may see more agents than buyers at first!

The agents may promise you quick sales, tell you horror stories of "The Fizz-bo That Never Sold," and give you their best sales pitch. You should be firm with the agents. Tell them that you've made up your mind to sell the home yourself.

In some cases, you may want to consider using some services of an agent, but not others. For instance, you may hire an agent to research comparable home sales and give advice on your list price. In this case, you may want to set a fee for the service. You may also let an agent prepare market reports for you. Some will do this for free in the hope that you'll eventually list your home with them.

Finally, you will have to work with buyers who are represented by an agent. A buyer with an agent is usually serious about buying a home and is usually prequalified. You don't want to turn away this type of buyer, even if you don't like the agent! Compensation for the buyer's agent should be discussed with the agent in advance.

# Hiring a Lawyer

Even if you don't hire anyone else, you'll definitely want to hire a lawyer. A lawyer can draw up or look over any contracts and ensure that your interests are protected. The lawyer can ensure that you do every-thing properly and legally.

When looking for a lawyer, ask for recommendations from friends, relatives, agents, and coworkers. Keep in mind that you'll want a lawyer who specializes in real estate. You don't want to use your sister, the divorce attorney, to handle the transaction.

You should understand up front the charges that you'll incur. The lawyer will most likely charge by the hour. You may draw up a contract that lists the hourly fee and spells out the services you want the lawyer to provide. You can expect the lawyer to prepare, obtain, and record documents; handle the mechanics of the property transfer; calculate any prorations; and receive and disburse money.

# Setting the Price

The single most important aspect of the sale of a home is the price. Setting the price is critical to a successful home sale. If you set the price too high, buyers may avoid your property. When a property sits and sits, it becomes a target for lowball bids. On the other hand, you don't want to price the home too low. You want to get the best deal possible! The best way to set the price of your home is to investigate sales of simi-lar homes in your area. This topic is covered in Chapter 19.

Comparable homes are of the same style (brick, frame, bungalow, two-storey), have the same number of bed-rooms and bathrooms, the same room types (dining room, rec room, living room), and are located in the same area. You can find the list price for homes by reading the local paper or by calling agents. You may also attend open houses of similar homes to see how yours compares.

**Set a Reasonable Price**

Be sure you have reason-able expectations when you price your home and plan your net proceeds. Many fizz-bos expect to pocket the entire commission savings. Savvy buyers may want to share in the savings.

To find the selling prices of homes, you'll have to do some research. These transactions are recorded at the provincial land titles office, so you can look through public records to find the information you need.

A co-operative agent will also give you this information. Or you may consider having your home appraised professionally.

## Figuring Your Net Proceeds

To prepare you for negotiations, determine your net proceeds from the sale of your home. Chapter 19 explains how to calculate this total. You should include the costs you incur in selling your home (advertising fees, legal costs, and so on). You should also determine the closing costs that pertain to your sale.

## Defining Acceptable Financial Terms

In addition to the list price, you should decide on the amount of down payment you (and the lender) will require.

# Marketing Your Home

Marketing the home means getting the attention of buyers. No matter how wonderful your home is, it won't sell unless buyers know it's available. This section discusses some strategies for getting noticed.

## Putting a Sign in Your Yard

One of the first steps in marketing your home is to put up a sign. A sign alerts neighbors that you're selling your home (and agents, too, so watch out!). It also tells others passing through the neighborhood that your home is for sale.

You can purchase a sign at a local hardware store. It should clearly say FOR SALE BY OWNER and should include space for your phone number. (Be sure to use a big, black marker so that your number is clearly visible.) When you put the sign in your yard, make sure that it can be seen easily, from both directions.

In addition to a yard sign, you may put up other signs around the neighborhood, including one on the main road into your neighborhood.

Be prepared for two things once the sign goes up. First, agents will flock to

**Hey! You Got a License for That Thing?**

Before you put up a sign, check your city laws or neighborhood ordinances pertaining to signs in your area. You may be limited in the size or type of sign you can put up.

you. Second, people will stop by, ring the doorbell, and ask to see your house. You can handle stop-bys by giving the buyers a tour, if it's convenient. Or you can give them an information sheet about your home (described later in this chapter) and schedule an appointment.

## Taking Out an Ad

In addition to signs, you should advertise your home in the local paper and perhaps in other publications. In most city papers, a large section is devoted to real estate in the weekend paper.

You don't have to take out a full-page ad to advertise your home. A small ad works perfectly well. Most buyers in the market for a home read all the small ads, so you don't have to worry about size. You should worry, however, about making your small ad stand out. You can do this by making the ad precise, descriptive, and inviting. A good ad should include the following:

➤ The price

➤ Your phone number

➤ Number of bedrooms and baths

➤ Style of home and condition of property

The ad should emphasize the benefits of your home, in a few words. What is its best feature? What do you like best about the house? What will buyers like best? After reading the ad, the buyer should want to visit your home.

You don't have to put the address in. You can schedule appointments and give callers the address. You should, however, put your address in if you hold an open house.

**Reach Out**

In addition to advertising in the paper, consider posting notices on bulletin boards in your local library or supermarket. The best way to decide where to advertise is to target your audience. Who is likely to want to purchase your home? How can you reach these buyers?

## Preparing Fact Sheets

When buyers visit your home, you want them to remember it after they leave. You should anticipate their questions and provide information in printed form. To do so, create a fact sheet that you can hand out during open houses and showings.

You can study the MLS listings used by agents for ideas of what to include (see Chapter 6). Also, visit open houses and collect their fact sheets. Here's some information to consider for your fact sheet:

➤ The address of your home.

➤ The list price.

➤ The best features of your home.

➤ The number of bedrooms and baths (the first thing a buyer wants to know).

➤ A description of other rooms in the house (living room, family room, dining room, office, and so on).

➤ Information about the age, construction (adobe, siding, block, brick, frame, stone, stucco, wood), style (bungalow, Cape Cod, Colonial, contemporary, Dutch Colonial, ranch, Spanish, split level, traditional, Tudor), and condition (move-in, needs work, as is).

➤ Information about the size of the house — number of storeys, total square footage, lot size, and room dimensions of living room, dining room, bedrooms, den, and other rooms.

➤ Any special features — fireplace, patio, pool, and so on.

➤ A description of the garage (if you have one).

➤ The types of major systems (heating, cooling, electricity, plumbing, water heater) and a record of utility costs.

➤ A list of appliances included with the house.

➤ Information about the neighborhood; for example, school district and annual taxes.

➤ Information about the current mortgage.

To make the fact sheet more appealing, you may want to include a photo of your home. You can also include a drawing of the layout or survey.

## Showing Your Home

If you've done a good job marketing your home, you'll have plenty of visitors. Expect, especially at first, a lot of snoop-

**Spread the Word**

Give fact sheets to your neighbors and coworkers and ask them to spread them around. They may know of someone in the market for a home.

ers (curious neighbors, agents, other potential fizz-bos comparing properties) and some potential buyers.

## Handling Sales Calls

You don't have an agent to schedule appointments, so you'll have to do this yourself, handling phone calls and greeting stop-bys.

For phone calls, you may want to write up a script so that you tell potential buyers everything they need to know. For instance, you should give a buyer directions to your home, a description of the home, and the list price.

You may also want to ask potential buyers a few questions. For instance, you can ask how the caller heard about the home to gauge the effectiveness of your marketing strategy. You should ask for the caller's name and phone number. You can write these down in your visitor log so that you know who has called and visited.

Then make an appointment to show the home at a time that's mutually convenient.

In some cases, potential buyers may just stop by and knock on the door. If it's convenient, you may show the home right then and there. If it isn't (if your four-year-old has just finger-painted himself and his sister, your spouse has decided to dismantle the dishwasher, and you're in the middle of giving your mother a home perm), you may just give the buyers a fact sheet and schedule an appointment for a more convenient time.

### Be Flexible

One of the benefits of having an agent is that you don't have to be available for showings during the day. If you're selling alone and you work, you may be able to schedule all your showings during the evenings, but be flexible. You may have to arrange for weekday showings as well.

## Showing Your House

When potential buyers visit your home, ask them to sign a visitor register and list their names and addresses. This will provide a record of visitors. You can keep your phone calls in the same or in a separate ledger.

To prepare for the showing, make sure the house is clean and clutter-free (see Chapter 17). Also, make sure the home is safe. Are the walkways clear? Is the dog put away? Any poisonous liquids sitting out on the table?

You may want to point out a few things of interest and then let the potential buyers wander through the house. Or you may want to accompany them on the tour. When you tag along, though, they may feel stifled. Be sure to put away any valuables, especially if you let the visitors tour the home alone.

During the tour, be prepared for questions about the area, your home, and financing. If you don't know the answers, say so. Don't lie and don't exaggerate.

## Holding Open Houses

In addition to scheduled showings, you may want to hold an open house or two. Open houses are traditionally held on Sunday afternoons.

If you plan an open house, advertise it in the paper. Also, make sure you have enough fact sheets on hand for visitors. Put up some additional signs in the neighborhood directing visitors to your home. As with regular showings, ask visitors to sign in.

## Helping the Buyer with Financing

One of the benefits of using an agent is that the agent can prequalify a buyer and can help a buyer obtain financing. Without an agent, you have to do this yourself.

First, you should prequalify anyone who's serious about making an offer. Just because Pam and Steve seem like a nice couple doesn't mean they have the money to buy your home. You shouldn't spend hours and hours working with a potential buyer only to find out that he can't afford the home.

To prequalify a person, you can purchase a buyer qualification form from an office supply company. Or you can draw up your own form with your lawyer's help. You need to know the person's income, job situation, current debt, and other information. Chapter 3 includes information on prequalifying and explains the ratios most lenders use. You can use this information to qualify a person yourself. If the person gets angry when you ask for financial information, be sure to explain why you need it. After you do so, the individual should understand.

You may help the person obtain financing once you've accepted an offer. An offer without financial backing isn't going to do you any good. To do this, you should be familiar with the different types of financing available. You can find this information in Chapter 12. You can also talk to local lenders. You may consider putting together an information sheet that lists the names of various lenders, maximum loan amounts, and fees. You can include this information along with your fact sheet.

# Negotiating an Offer

An agent serves as a go-between, discussing offers with potential buyers and their agent and then relaying that information to you.

Without the agent, you have to negotiate face-to-face with the potential buyers and possibly with their agent. Put on your poker face and leave your thin skin at home.

## Be Prepared

Face-to-face negotiating is tough. You have to be prepared for negative comments about your home. If you take the comments personally, the process will be stressful. If you understand that the comments are probably just part of the buyer's strategy to get more favorable terms, you can prepare yourself to handle any objections.

You may want to role play with your spouse or a friend. Have that person say the bad things to you about your house — even if they aren't true. "Well, the roof needs to be repaired. The kitchen tile is the worst. And who picked the wallpaper in the living room? It looks like soup!" You can then counter with "The roof was repaired last year. The price takes into consideration the kitchen tile, and if you don't like the wallpaper, you can select something that you do like."

You should also determine your bottom line. Knowing the price and terms you'll accept can help you when you have to evaluate offers.

## Drawing Up Offers

If your buyers are working with an agent, the agent may help them draw up an offer. If not, they may have a lawyer do the work. Or the buyers may come to you with their own purchase agreement.

If, on the other hand, the buyers don't have anyone to help them with an offer, and need help, you can help them with a contract form purchased from an office supply store. If the standard contract isn't to your liking, you can ask your lawyer to draw up a contract.

## Reviewing Offers

When a buyer has an offer, you should schedule an appointment at your home. When you receive the offer, thank the buyers and ask for time to review it. Usually a sales contract stipulates a time for a response (24 to 48 hours is typical).

During that response time, you can examine the offer. What price are the buyers offering? What terms? How does this compare to what you expected? Reviewing offers and making counteroffers are covered in Chapter 20.

The offer-counteroffer process can continue until someone withdraws an offer or until both parties agree to the same offer. When you've both signed the same agreement, you have successfully sold your home!

# Closing on the House

The final stage in buying and selling a home is the closing. At the closing, you exchange money and keys, and you sign more documents than you ever imagined.

To handle the closing, you need a lawyer, who will prepare a settlement sheet. He'll need the original purchase contract to start.

Using the contract as a blueprint, the lawyer draws up the instructions for you and the buyers. (Chapter 21 describes the function of the lawyer.) You should be prepared to carry out all the instructions the lawyer gives you and to provide any information the lawyer needs (deed, mortgage documents, property tax statements, survey, and so on).

The lawyer will not reveal information to other parties and will not revise the instructions without authorization by you and the buyer.

Before the closing, the lawyer will let you and the buyers know the closing costs that must be paid and by whom. He will also calculate any prorations. At the closing, the lawyer will ensure that all the proper documents have been prepared and signed. The lawyer will arrange for your original loan(s) to be paid off and for the new deed to be recorded. After the deed has been recorded, the lawyer will release to you your hard-earned check for any proceeds on the sale of your home.

# Knowing When to Call It Quits

If you've had your home on the market for a while and haven't sold it, take a second look. Why hasn't the property sold? Chapter 20 lists some reasons why a home may not sell, including the price, the market, the terms, and the condition. Review these items and try to pinpoint the problem.

Consider using an agent, especially if it turns out that exposure is the main problem (getting buyers to the house) or if the property market is cold. When you set out to sell your home, set a time limit. Say "If I haven't sold my home in 6 (8, 10?) months, I'll get an agent." When you reach your deadline, hire an agent.

Finally, if the market is so slow or interest rates are so high that you're not getting any acceptable offers, consider taking your house off the market for a while.

# The Least You Need to Know

If you have a knack for sales and an understanding of the real estate market, you may want to forego paying an agent a 6% commission, and sell your home yourself.

➤ Be sure you understand what's involved in selling your home. You may want to hire consultants — for example, an agent — to help with some but not all of the steps.

➤ The most important aspect of selling a home is setting the price. To come up with a price, compare similar homes in the area. You may want to hire an agent to help you with pricing.

➤ To get your home noticed put a FOR SALE BY OWNER sign in your yard and advertise in the local daily paper and neighborhood weeklies.

➤ Create a fact sheet about your home to hand out to potential buyers when they visit.

➤ Negotiating face-to-face with a potential buyer can be tough. Be prepared to deal with criticism and objections, and know your bottom line.

➤ The final step in selling a home is the closing. You should hire a lawyer to prepare the instructions for the closing, ensure all documents are prepared and properly signed, and to hold all the money and distribute it when the deal is complete.

**Never spend your money before
you have it.**

—Thomas Jefferson

# Index